Δ The Triangle Papers: 59

ENGAGING WITH RUSSIA
The Next Phase

A Report to
The Trilateral Commission

RODERIC LYNE
European Author

STROBE TALBOTT
North American Author

KOJI WATANABE
Pacific Asian Author

The Trilateral Commission
Washington, Paris, Tokyo
2006

The Trilateral Commission was formed in 1973 by private citizens of Europe, Japan, and North America to foster closer cooperation among these three democratic industrialized regions on common problems. It seeks to improve public understanding of such problems, to support proposals for handling them jointly, and to nurture habits and practices of working together. The European group has widened with the ongoing enlargement of the European Union. The Japanese group has widened into a Pacific Asia group. The North American group now includes members from Canada, Mexico, and the United States.

The Trilateral Commission

www.trilateral.org

1156 15th Street, NW
Washington, DC 20005

5, Rue de Téhéran
75008 Paris, France

Japan Center for International Exchange
4-9-17 Minami-Azabu
Minato-ku
Tokyo 106, Japan

Contents

The Authors

Sir Roderic Lyne served as the British ambassador to Russia from January 2000 until August 2004, when he retired from the Foreign and Commonwealth Office after 34 years. He now works as a consultant, company director, and lecturer and continues to visit Russia frequently. He also served as the UK's permanent representative to the World Trade Organization and the United Nations and other international organizations in Geneva from 1997 to 2000 and as the private secretary to the prime minister, responsible for foreign and European affairs, defense and security, and Northern Ireland, from 1993 to 1996.

In his earlier career, Roderic Lyne served in the USSR in the early 1970s and again from 1987 to 1990; he was head of the Soviet (subsequently Eastern) Department of the Foreign and Commonwealth Office from 1990 to 1993. His other assignments included service at the UK mission to the United Nations in New York and at the British embassy in Senegal; as an assistant private secretary to the foreign secretary; and on secondment to British Gas plc and to the Royal Institute of International Affairs at Chatham House. He is a history graduate of Leeds University and has been awarded honorary doctorates by Leeds, Kingston, and Heriot-Watt Universities.

Strobe Talbott assumed the presidency of the Brookings Institution in July 2002 after a career in journalism, government, and academe. His immediate previous post was founding director of the Yale Center for the Study of Globalization. He served in the U.S. Department of State from 1993 to 2001, first as ambassador-at-large and special adviser to the secretary of state for the new independent states of the former Soviet Union, then for seven years as deputy secretary of state.

Mr. Talbott entered government after 21 years with *Time* magazine. As a reporter, he covered Eastern Europe, the State Department, and the White House; then he became Washington bureau chief, editor-at-large, and foreign affairs columnist. In addition to translating two volumes of Nikita Khrushchev's memoirs, he has written nine books including, most recently, *Engaging India: Diplomacy, Democracy and the Bomb* (2004) and *The Russia Hand* (2002). He is currently working on a book about global governance, to be published in 2007. He was educated at Hotchkiss, Yale, and Oxford.

Koji Watanabe is a senior fellow at the Japan Center for International Exchange and was Japan's ambassador to Russia from 1993 to 1996 and ambassador to Italy from 1992 to 1993. He was also deputy minister for foreign affairs, sherpa for the G-7 Houston and London summits of 1991 and 1990, and he served as Japan's cochair of the U.S.-Japan Structural Impediments Initiative Talks. Ambassador Watanabe joined the Ministry of Foreign Affairs upon graduating from the University of Tokyo, and he served as director-general of the Information Analysis, Research, and Planning Bureau and of the Economic Affairs Bureau. He was a visiting fellow at the Woodrow Wilson School at Princeton University in 1957–58 and at the Center for International Affairs at Harvard University in 1973–74. His other overseas posts have included counselor at the Japanese embassy in Saigon (1974–76), minister at the Japanese embassy in Beijing (1981–84), and ambassador to Saudi Arabia (1988–89).

Ambassador Watanabe is president of The Japan Forum and was formerly a member of the National Public Safety Commission, member of the board of governors of the Asia-Europe Foundation (ASEF), and executive adviser to the Japan Business Federation (Nippon Keidanren). Ambassador Watanabe was the Japanese coauthor (with Sherman W. Garnett and Alexander Rahr) of the Trilateral task force report, *The New Central Asia: In Search of Stability* (2000).

The Trilateral Process

Although only the authors are responsible for the analysis and conclusions, they have been aided in their work by extensive consultations. These consultations embraced many government officials, experts, and others in the Trilateral countries and included discussion at the European regional meeting of the Commission in Madrid in October 2005 and at the North American regional meeting in Montreal in November 2005. Within Europe, consultations were held in London, Paris, Milan, Berlin, Warsaw, and Kiev as well as at the EU institutions and at NATO headquarters in Brussels. The authors greatly appreciate the guidance, cooperation, and hospitality extended to them during these consultations by national and regional groups of the Trilateral Commission.

The consultations concluded with a joint visit by the coauthors to Moscow on February 13–16, 2006. The authors would like to express their appreciation to Minister of Foreign Affairs of the Russian Federation Sergei Lavrov, Secretary of the Security Council Igor Ivanov, Head of the Federal Atomic Energy Agency Sergei Kiriyenko, Chairman of the Russian Chamber of Commerce and Industry Yevgeniy Primakov; and Chairman of the Foreign Affairs Committee of the State Duma Konstantin Kosachev for generously making time available during a busy period. The authors were greatly indebted to Chairman of the Council on Foreign and Defense Policy Sergei Karaganov for arranging their program in Moscow, with the invaluable assistance of Alexander Belkin for convening a seminar on Russia's external relations and security and for his hospitality and expert advice. They would like to thank President Yegor Gaidar of the Institute for Economics in Transition who kindly convened a seminar on the economy, and the British, American, and Japanese ambassadors, respectively Anthony Brenton, William J. Burns, and Issei Nomura, for their kind hospitality The authors are likewise grateful for the introductory briefing held at the Moscow Carnegie Center. In the course of the visit to Moscow, the authors benefited from the views of a wide range of politicians, officials, and experts. They are grateful to all for their frankness and friendship.

In addition to their oral consultations, the authors have drawn on many written sources. Some are identified in footnotes, but, as this is not an academic treatise, the authors have not appended a bibliography or full list of sources. They have drawn extensively on reports and documents from the IMF, IBRD, OECD, IEA, OSCE, Council of Europe, and European Commission; and they have benefited from studies, papers, and articles published by, among others, the Carnegie Endowment for International Peace (including the work of the outstanding Carnegie Center in Moscow), the Council on Foreign Relations (New York), the Brookings Institution (Washington), the Japan Center for International Exchange (Tokyo), the Council on Foreign and Defense Policy (Moscow), the Higher School of Economics (Moscow), the New Economic School (Moscow), the Centre for European Reform (London), the Center for European Policy Studies (Brussels), the European Round Table of Industrialists (Brussels), the Royal Institute of International Affairs (London), the International Institute for Strategic Studies (London), the Institute for Security Studies—European Union (Paris), Deutsche Gesellschaft für Auswärtige Politik (Berlin), Istituto per gli Studi di Politica Internazionale (Milan), Institut français des relations internationales (Paris), Goldman Sachs, Standard & Poor's, and the PBN company. Among the books that have provided invaluable background (many of which are acknowledged in the text), Professor Anthony Cross's 1971 compilation, *Russia under Western Eyes, 1517–1825* has been a rich source of historical quotations.

Acknowledgments

The brunt of the labor of organizing the consultations and shepherding the authors through to the conclusion of this exercise was borne by the inexhaustibly patient and wise European director of the Trilateral Commission, Paul Révay, assisted by Karine Fargier. He was strongly supported in Europe by the European deputy chairman, Andrzej Olechowski in Warsaw; Bernhard May, secretary general of the German group; Ernesto Vellano, secretary general of the Italian group; in the United States by Michael J. O'Neil, North American director (who supervised publication of the report); and in Japan by Tadashi Yamamoto, Pacific Asia director. The report would not have seen the light of day without the encouragement and humane coercion applied by the three directors.

Finally, the authors would like to express their gratitude for the herculean labors in turning crude manuscript into finished product of Mandy Lyne and Lorraine Lockley in the UK; Sue Ellen Parrott, Andreas Xenachis, Fiona Hill, Clifford Gaddy, Carlos Pascual, and Erik Berglof in the United States; and Hideko Katsumata, Kim Ashizawa, Hifumi Tajima, Hyoma Ito at the JCIE in Japan, and Kazuhiko Togo at Princeton University.

1

Introduction

> A Nation of Inconsistence, Contradiction and Paradox, Uniting in Themselves the Most Opposite Extremes
>
> —Sir George Macartney
> *An Account of Russia,* 1768

"U Rossii yest' svoya spetsifika," Russians are wont to say. "Russia is unique, Russia has its own distinctive character."

Every nation, of course, has its own peculiarities and distinctive facets. Down the ages, however, Russia has suffered more than most from attempts simply to superimpose Western values and to transplant Western experience into a country that has followed its own route, on the fringes of Europe and Asia, Christendom and Islam, ever since Prince Vladimir of Kievan Rus chose the Orthodox Church of Byzantium in preference to Catholicism or Islam just over a thousand years ago. This is a nation that

> in the course of the second Christian millennium . . . rose out of obscure origins and inhospitable surroundings to build the largest land empire of all time and one of the world's great cultures.[1]

The debate between Slavophiles and Westerners has a 300-year history and continues to this day, but even the Westerners within Russia react sharply to those who choose to lecture them about the West's superior wisdom and civilization while taking little account of Russia's circumstances, above all of her history, geography, climate, and ethnic composition. A minister in the Russian government put it to us emphatically that "we don't just have to follow the policies of the West."

---

1 James H. Billington, *The Face of Russia: Anguish, Aspiration, and Achievement in Russian Culture* (New York: TV Books, 1999).

Russia certainly felt special to our small group from the Trilateral Commission when we visited Moscow in February 2006. The temperature had just risen from below minus 30º Celsius to a balmy minus 15° or minus 20º. The domes of the capital were gleaming in sun reflected off fresh snow. The town was buzzing, full of foreign visitors even in February, showing the glitz and the self-confidence of the wealth washing through it: many fine old buildings restored; some, sadly, demolished and replaced with modern architecture of eclectic styles and varying attractiveness.

And, from morning to night, people opened their doors and wanted to talk. There was no sense of the gray oppressiveness that we all remembered from the past. Strong opinions, including about our own countries, were thrust at us, but with good humor and friendship.

Russia has always been a source of fascination to foreigners and a challenge to those who seek to understand it or to involve themselves in its affairs. Long before Winston Churchill coined his overused aphorism about Russia's mysterious nature, Sir George Macartney, who had spent two years in Moscow negotiating a trade agreement and was seeking to explain Russia to outsiders, wrote in 1768:

> [T]ho' we may amuse ourselves with the speculation of second causes, we must still remain ignorant of the first: we are bewildered in our pursuit, and at the moment we think the case within our reach, it mocks our eagerness and vanishes from our view.

There have been times during our consultations in Russia, elsewhere in Europe, in North America, and in Asia when we have thought the case within our reach, but Russia remains a hugely contradictory place, where forming a balanced view is an elusive task.

It is a place where one meets some of the world's most bullish businessmen—Russian and multinational—and most bearish economists and political analysts. It is a country that has benefited greatly from six years of political stability and where enormous power has been consolidated by the current leadership—but one where there is deep uncertainty about the future, power is fragile, and the leadership displays a sense of insecurity; a nation that is enjoying degrees of freedom unprecedented in its history, but pervaded by creeping self-censorship and renewed fear of the various organs of internal security and control; an economy and a fast growing market that has been one of the success stories of this decade but one whose growth will be hard to sustain in the next decade if current policies persist.

> Moscow is in everything extraordinary; as well in disappointing expectation, as in surpassing it; in causing wonder and derision, pleasure and regret.
>
> —Edward Clarke
> *Travels in Various Countries,* 1810

Central to these contradictions is that the Russian Federation is in the throes of not one, but three, simultaneous processes of transition in what is, by land area, by far the world's largest country: the transition from the second superpower, an imperial power directly or indirectly ruling 350 million people, to a middling or regional power with a declining population of just over 140 million; the transition from a collapsed autarkic command economy to a market economy integrating into the world economic system; and the transition from Communist dictatorship, ideology, and control of society to a new political order, the eventual shape of which remains to be determined. While Russia's standing as a global power is in decline, its economy is on the rise: in simplistic terms, the country is going down and up at the same time. These changes have come with great suddenness. For a people with a long history and a deep sense of national pride, the changes have been traumatic.

For Russia's leaders, the triple transition presents daunting problems. As one minister put it to us: 15 years after the collapse of Communism, Russia is still in "search" mode for her political model. Another stressed that, in 2000, the country had been at risk of disintegration: it had been vital to reestablish unified systems of law and governance, and a greater degree of control from the center. Several interlocutors, citing Palestine, Iran, and Georgia as examples, underlined the risks of introducing full democracy in a society that was not prepared for it. One likened the West's "export of democracy" to Trotsky's "export of revolution."

On the liberal side, the situation was described variously as rule by clans ("from Gosplan to Gosclan"); the restoration, not of Communism, but of Soviet bureaucracy; and weak authoritarianism with some of the external attributes of democracy. Most of those whom we met expressed concern about the potency of nationalism as a force within Russia, and the risk that, were a crisis to occur, a government of the Far Right could be elected (although there is a conflicting argument, backed by some polling evidence, that the extent of extreme nationalism tends to be exaggerated). Some argue that the risk of populist extremism justifies a policy of limiting democracy ("managed democracy," in the Kremlin's phrase); others argue that the risk exists precisely because of the absence of strong and independent democratic institutions.

One sage and experienced figure summed up this confusion of conflicting, reasoned opinions as a reflection of the problem of finding a proper balance between governability and the basic democratic rights of the people. This is not a problem unique to Russia; nor is it a new question. In his account of Russia in 1768, Macartney observed: "to despotism Russia owes her greatness and dominion; so that if ever the monarchy becomes more limited, she will lose her power and strength, in proportion as she advances in moral virtue and civil improvement."

The prevailing mood of those we consulted outside Russia might best be summed up as puzzlement and disappointment. There was disappointment that efforts from within and without to engage Russia, proclamations of "strategic partnership," and Russia's accession to the chairmanship of the Group of Eight (G-8) had not led to closer relationships. There was puzzlement that the strong trend toward modernization within Russia from 2000 to 2003 had halted or gone into reverse. The growth of the Russian economy over the past six years, the development of business, including increased foreign trade and investment, and the rising levels of prosperity were of course seen everywhere as a very positive factor; but there was also concern at the direction of the economy and that an opportunity to diversify and establish it on a modern and competitive basis was being missed. Russia's stability after the turmoil of the 1990s is another important positive factor; but here, too, concerns were expressed both inside and outside Russia that emphasis on control could lead to sclerosis and brittleness and could act against the development of a stable society over the long term.

In the report that follows, we seek to explore these issues of transition more fully. The report is neither an academic study of Russia nor a polemic. All three coauthors have devoted significant parts of their working lives to studying and dealing with the Soviet Union and Russia, and they have lived and worked there at different periods from the 1960s to the present day. They have not only deep ties with the country and affection for it, but many close friendships there. The report represents the sum of their personal views. It reflects their personal desire to see a great country and its talented peoples succeed in overcoming the legacy of a difficult past and in building a stable, prosperous, and harmonious society within Russia and strong partnerships beyond.

This report aims to make a contribution to public debate, not by downplaying problems, but by assessing them in context, in a candid and balanced way, and by looking for constructive ways forward. It seeks to understand the development of the Russian Federation in the post-Soviet era, including the development of new processes in politics and society, of a market economy, and of new external relationships; to explore the choices facing Russia and the ways in which the country might develop over the next generation; and to look at the implications for Russia's partners.

Chapter 2 looks at the legacy inherited from the 1990s (when the Trilateral Commission last surveyed Russia). Chapters 3 and 4 assess the main trends and policies under the current administration. Chapter 5 examines Russia's role in the G-8 and her relations with the United States. In chapter 6 we look at the evolution of Russia's relations within the European continent and in chapter 7, at the parallel processes in Asia. In chapter 8, we draw some conclusions about the direction in which Russia is heading and the impediments to progress. In chapter 9 we offer recommendations on the approach of the Trilateral countries.

2

Post-Communist Russia: From Yeltsin to Putin

Freedom. This is Boris Yeltsin's great historical achievement.

—President Vladimir V. Putin
Press conference, January 31, 2006

Yeltsin's First Term: The 1995 Trilateral Commission Report

The Trilateral Commission last commissioned a study on Russian 11 years ago. The report, *Engaging Russia,* was presented by Robert Blackwill, Sir Rodric Braithwaite, and Akihiko Tanaka in April 1995. It provides a useful starting point for the present study.

Engaging Russia described a "political, economic, and above all a psychological and cultural revolution." The end of the Cold War had been followed by a natural euphoria in East and West but also by a falling off of interest in Russia by the outside world and a new Russian assertiveness in the mid-1990s over such issues as Bosnia and Iraq. Moreover,

> . . . the uncertainties of Russian domestic politics have also revived fears of a return to the authoritarianism and expansionism of the past. The mood between Moscow and Washington has become more tetchy. The ghost of the old confrontation has not been fully laid to rest. Russia's closest neighbours, such as Poland and the Baltic States with their bitter memories of the past, continue to view Russia with intense suspicion . . . The reaction of most Russians to the collapse of the Soviet empire is ambiguous.

The fundamental question, in the view of the coauthors, was whether Russia could escape from her historical burden—or was the revolution that started in 1985 bound to end in failure, as had happened to earlier attempts to reform Russia? Could Russia surmount "powerful ancient predispositions" and become "an enduring partner of the industrial democracies?"

The coauthors were concerned that a combination of an authoritarian past, weak or nonexistent democratic institutions, domestic economic turbulence and hardship, political extremism, instability in border areas, and the growing conviction that Russia's national interests were in important respects sharply different from those of the West would produce many policies from Moscow that would trouble Trilateral governments. At the extreme, this could even lead to pressure in some quarters for "neo-containment policies." They stressed that the transition would take a long time:

> A revolution as profound as the one which now grips Russia will inevitably involve serious reverses as well as significant advance. It cannot be completed in years or even decades. The Russian people will take generations to rid themselves of the incubus of the autocratic, militarized and introverted state traditions of the past, and replace them with liberal political and economic habits more suited to the modern world and Russia's place in it. For the next ten, twenty or fifty years, therefore, Russia is likely to be in a state of greater or lesser turmoil . . . But the prize remains what it was in that time of euphoria: to engage Russia fully in the family of democratic nations.

At the time of the 1995 report, President Boris Yeltsin still had a government of a liberal hue, and he had credit in his account for democratic achievement. Gaidar's government had liberalized prices in the early 1990s, cut military procurement and industrial subsidies, and reduced the budget deficit. Inflation had spiraled to a frightening 2,300 percent in 1992 but had reduced to 240 percent in 1994 and was on a downward course. Privatization had advanced, in a rough-and-ready way, with over 60 percent of gross domestic product (GDP) in 1994 produced by the private sector. Commercial banks and exchanges had opened, and foreigners were beginning to invest in a small way in Russia (although the inflow was mostly offset by capital flight). For a while after 1991, Russia enjoyed a fairly transparent system of parliamentary government. Free media had developed. The KGB had been divided into discrete agencies, and its prestige had fallen dramatically after the 1991 coup d'état and the power of the organs of internal security was much reduced (although it kept huge numbers on the payroll: the report quoted a figure of 140,000 for the counterintelligence service, the FSK, now renamed FSB).

> [President Yeltsin] has not always identified himself personally with a coherent long-term program of reform, preferring to keep his distance in order to preserve his freedom of maneuver.
>
> The FSK [now FSB] is once again appealing to the paranoia which is never far from the surface in Russia by blaming many of the country's ills on foreign intrigue.
>
> One of the main motives behind the popular call in Russia today for a strong hand in government has been the fear that change will lead to the unleashing of the elemental forces of popular rebellion.
>
> —Sir Rodric Braithwaite
> *Engaging Russia*
> Report to the Trilateral Commission, 1995

However, the early 1990s had been a period of enormous turmoil in society, the economy, the regions, and politics. By 1995, internal gales were blowing liberalism off course. After his confrontation with the Russian Supreme Soviet in 1993, Yeltsin had secured the electorate's approval for a new constitution that greatly enhanced the powers of the president. The constitution was criticized for "opening the possibility of a new dictatorship under one of Yeltsin's successors." Power shifted to the Kremlin—to the presidential entourage and the unelected

Security Council, meeting in secret—and increasingly was exercised through presidential decrees. Another turning point was Yeltsin's ill-fated decision to invade Chechnya in the autumn of 1994. The campaign was managed abysmally, was unpopular within Russia, and caused a breach with Russia's Western partners. Tensions between the West and Russia were further exacerbated by the Bosnian conflict and by moves to bring the first former Warsaw Pact countries (Poland, Hungary, and the Czech Republic) into NATO.

One of the conclusions of the 1995 report is particularly resonant 11 years on:

> There is a reasonable chance that the reform process in Russia will continue to lurch forward, despite all the risk and pain which the country will encounter over the next few years. The most likely alternative would be a move toward "mild authoritarianism": some version of the "Pinochet solution" . . . It would involve a further concentration of power in the hands of the Presidency, a further diminution in the powers of parliament, an attempt to increase the state's direct control over the economy, and doubtless some curb on the freedom of the press . . . But there would not be a massive reduction in the scope for ordinary people to say what they think, to pursue their private commercial interests, or to travel abroad. Such a regime would no doubt remain committed, at least in theory, to some version of market economics. It would not preclude a resumption—perhaps quite rapidly—of progress toward political democracy. But in the meanwhile Trilateral countries would find it much harder to treat such a regime as an acceptable equal partner.

Yeltsin's Second Term and Handover to Putin (1996–2000)

Boris Yeltsin's second term was a bad and humiliating time for Russia. The brave, strong, and charismatic figure who had led Russia out of Communism and empire in the early 1990s presented a sad spectacle: ailing, absent for long periods, capable only of short bursts of vigor, and in the clutches of a small circle of cronies. As Lilia Shevtsova put it:

> It was hard to discern, in the shell of a man left by the late 1990s, the Boris Yeltsin who had ridden the democratic wave in the late 1980s and the beginning of the 1990s and who could elicit unconditional support from crowds merely by his presence. The leader who had made his mission Russia's return to Europe and its transformation into a flourishing democratic state ended up a politician completely dependent on his Kremlin servants, stooping to primitive intrigue and manipulation to survive . . . As Yeltsin grew weaker physically, the ostensibly superpresidential system became obviously disabled, devolving into a half-hearted Impotent Omnipotence.[1]

Many Russians sum up Yeltsin's second term in a single word: chaos. It was certainly a period that both tarnished the cause of reform and left a difficult legacy for his successor.

Yeltsin had dedicated himself to the defeat of Communism. In this, he was partially successful. The Communist Party remained, and remains, a substantial, organized force in Russian politics; but after Yeltsin's defeat of Zyuganov in the 1996 presidential election, any likelihood that Russia would return to Communist ideology or a command economy appeared gone. In subsequent elections, the Kremlin seems to have enjoyed a de facto accommodation with Zyuganov's Communists. The Communist Party helps to present an appearance of pluralism and, in a sanitized way, to represent a body of the Russian electorate on the Left but without threatening the Kremlin's control or mounting a serious challenge. The party's leaders and Duma deputies appear content to live within in this comfort zone and to enjoy the perks of acquiescence.

Yeltsin's "victory" over Communism was achieved at the expense of democracy and of the economy. His reelection in 1996 was secured only through the financial support and control of television by a small group of magnates—subsequently dubbed the "oligarchs." Under the loans-for-shares scheme, first presented by Potanin, Khodorkovsky, and Smolensky to the Russian Cabinet on March 31, 1995, this group of oligarchs was able to secure control of some of Russia's most valuable

1 Lilia Shevtsova, *Putin's Russia* (Washington, D.C.: Carnegie Endowment for International Peace, 2003).

assets, including oil fields, at ludicrously low prices in exchange for political support.[2]

Subsequently, at Davos in February 1996, the oligarchs temporarily set aside personal feuds and formed a pact to ensure Yeltsin's reelection. This deal (justly described by one author as a "Faustian bargain") was seen by liberal reformers in Yeltsin's government as necessary and justifiable in order to keep out the Communist challenger, Zyuganov. Western Governments and commentators, in their huge relief at the removal of the specter of a Zyuganov presidency, for the most part turned a blind eye to the manipulation of the election. With the wisdom of hindsight, Russia paid a high price for this result.

The Faustian pact ultimately did not work to the benefit of the liberals who had colluded with it. Yeltsin drifted further away from democracy, back to the Russian tradition of the all-powerful Kremlin. He fell deeper into the hands and pockets of courtiers who helped to ensure his maintenance in office—notably the sinister figure of Boris Berezovsky, with Roman Abramovich at his side and Tatyana Dyachenko acting as a link to her father, the president. The Parliament was too weak to resist or check those acting in the name of the frequently absent president. No further significant progress was made in promoting reform, adopting desperately needed legislation, or modernizing the country. While they lasted, liberal ministers and advisers had their hands full managing crises and fighting fires. During Yeltsin's final two years reform and modernization measures were mostly jettisoned. The liberals shared the blame for the failure to develop checks and balances for they had not wanted to be impeded when pushing through reform during their ascendancy in the early 1990s. Neither had the liberals taken the time to sell their policies to the country, to build grassroots support, or to develop effective political parties.

The transfer of power from Yeltsin to Putin in the second half of 1999 was an even more heavily managed exercise in manipulated "democracy." After a process of cogitation and selection behind closed doors, Yeltsin had nominated Vladimir Putin as prime minister in August 1999—Yeltsin's seventh change of prime minister in eight years.

---

2 The story of the loans-for-shares scam and the acquisition of power by the oligarchs has been told in graphic detail in several books, including *Sale of the Century,* by Chrystia Freeland; *The Oligarchs,* by David E. Hoffman; and *Godfather of the Kremlin,* by Paul Klebnikov—who was murdered in Moscow in 2004.

Putin had been heading the FSB, the internal security agency. Since leaving his career in the KGB in 1991, he had served as a deputy governor of St. Petersburg and in middle-ranking Kremlin positions. He was known to insiders for his efficient and loyal service, first to Governor Sobchak in St. Petersburg and then to President Yeltsin, but he had never been viewed by his peers as a candidate for the top. He himself seemed surprised by his appointment. To the public he was a complete unknown. He had no political background or following.

> [T]his intense desire to be great, to be seen as great, and to be treated by others as great lies deep in the Russian psyche . . .
>
> [M]any of Soviet Communism's habits of thought and standard operating procedures remain widespread throughout the national security agencies of the Russian government today.
>
> [F]or the next several years at a minimum, Russian domestic politics will be a seriously negative and not a reinforcing factor in attempts to improve the quality of Russia's relations with the West.
>
> —Robert Blackwill
> *Engaging Russia*
> Report to the Trilateral Commission, 1995

Three factors were critical in propelling an untried candidate with no profile and no platform from obscurity into the presidency in a mere five months. The first was the power of the presidential office. Although Yeltsin was by now discredited and unpopular, he was nevertheless able to use his office to select and anoint his successor in an entirely personal way. Yeltsin's blessing did not guarantee Putin's accession, but it gave him a massive advantage. In many countries, the designated successor would have inherited the unpopularity of the incumbent. In Russia, becoming crown prince gave him the aura and the machinery of the court and of power.

Second, whether by chance or design, Putin soon acquired a profile. A week before Putin's nomination to the premiership, Chechen separatists invaded the neighboring republic of Dagestan. In the first half of September a second incursion followed, and apartment buildings were bombed, with heavy loss of life in Dagestan, Moscow, and Volgodonsk. The bombings were blamed on Chechen terrorists, although this has never been proved conclusively. On September 30, 1999, Russian forces launched a full-scale operation to put down the Chechen rebellion, scoring some easy successes in the first month and occupying the republic's northern lowlands. This was seen from the outset as Putin's war, and at first it was popular with the Russian public. The Khasavyurt agreement, negotiated by General Lebed at Yeltsin's behest to end the previous conflict in 1996, had surrendered control of Chechnya to the separatists. For three years Chechen separatists thumbed their noses at Moscow (to the extent of abducting in March 1999 the Russian deputy minister of the interior, General Shpigun, at Grozny airport and murdering him). The counterattack directed by Putin seemed at the time to end a long period of humiliation. Politically, it gave Putin the image with the public of a strong decision maker and man of action—someone they yearned for after the enfeebled vacillation of Yeltsin's latter years.

Third, rival contenders for the throne had to be seen off. The threat this time came not from the Communists but from two veteran heavyweights—Yuri Luzhkov, the mayor of Moscow, and Yevgeniy Primakov, who had served Yeltsin as head of the foreign intelligence service, as foreign minister, and as prime minister. They had combined forces to form the Fatherland/All-Russia bloc (OVR). Luzhkov had a roguish charisma and was credited with visible improvements to the capital; Primakov supplied vast experience, gravitas, and a wide appeal to innate Russian conservatism. In a fair presidential election, a Primakov-Luzhkov ticket (in whatever combination) would have been a serious challenge to the neophyte prime minister. The battle was decided, however, before campaigning could begin for the presidential election scheduled for mid-2000. Using, and abusing, ownership of television (as they had during Yeltsin's reelection campaign in 1996), the circle of businesspeople around Yeltsin led by Berezovsky orchestrated a series of no-holds-barred media attacks on Luzhkov and Primakov. This undermined OVR's performance in the December 1999 Duma election, as well as gave Luzhkov and Primakov a foretaste of what to expect, should they presume to challenge Yeltsin's nominee for the presidency. The Communist Party won the largest number of seats in the Duma (114 out of 450, with 26 percent of the votes). Among the array of non-Communist parties, however, the "Unity" bloc cobbled together by Yeltsin's team took second place with 73 seats, ahead of OVR's 66. Putin also enjoyed the support of the right-of-center liberal grouping, the Union of Right Forces (SPS), which won 29 seats.

Putin's campaign now had momentum, but there was still half a year to go until the presidential election was due, and much could happen in that time. The Yeltsin team then played a trump card. Yeltsin resigned dramatically on December 31, 1999. Putin, as prime minister, automatically became acting president. The election was brought forward to March 26. The severely bruised Luzhkov and Primakov took the hint and did not run (a decision that was to prove beneficial to their health during Putin's presidency). This left the dog-eared and charisma-free Communist leader, Zyuganov, as the only credible challenger in a field of 11—but this time he did not have any realistic chance of winning. Russia had moved on since 1995–96, but Zyuganov had not.

The election became a coronation of the man already installed on the Kremlin throne, with interest focused on whether Putin would secure the 50 percent of the votes needed for a first-round victory (achieved by Yeltsin in 1991 but not in 1996). In the event, Putin scored 52.94 percent (though some have claimed that shenanigans in various regions helped him over the bar), while Zyuganov registered 29.21 percent. The popularity Putin had acquired as prime minister and acting president, not just through Chechnya but also through his personal appeal, played a major part in his victory. But it was also Yeltsin's final victory: he and his inner circle had determined in August 1999 that this was the result they wanted in order to protect (they hoped—mistakenly in Berezovsky's case) their own positions, and they had used low tactics to help bring it about.

Achievements and Legacy of Boris Yeltsin's Presidency

In other ways, too, Russia failed to advance in a democratic direction or to build stronger institutions during Yeltsin's second term. Even in feeble hands, the presidency remained the only institution with real strength. During his premiership from September 1998 to May 1999,

Primakov, as head of the Council of Ministers, tried to develop a degree of independence from the Kremlin, but he paid the price with his job. After the defeat of the Supreme Soviet in 1993 and the enactment of the new constitution, the Duma functioned as a querulous but largely impotent legislature that the president could ignore or bypass as he chose. Russia did not develop mature and meaningful political parties based on grassroots membership.

The Communist Party had a national organization and a solid core of voters, but it failed to update itself or adapt to the new environment by becoming a recognizably democratic party (as other Communist parties had done with some success in Eastern Europe). Zhirinovsky's Liberal Democratic Party seems, fortunately, to have peaked as a political force in 1993, when it finished first in the party-list poll with 23 percent of the vote (against 6 percent in 1999 and a 2.7 percent vote for Zhirinovsky in the 2000 presidential election). The party is neither liberal nor democratic, but instead seeks to exploit democracy in order to appeal to the basest instincts in the electorate. Genuine liberals and democrats signally failed to work together in a common cause by forging a united and cohesive party or movement. The SPS contained some exceptionally able people but was tainted by association with big business and was ambivalent in its relationship with the Kremlin. Yabloko also had talent, and was more effective in building a grassroots organization, but on its own it was never likely to be more than a small minority party. It paid a heavy price at the polls in 1999 for Yavlinsky's principled stand against the war in Chechnya.

On a more positive note, Russians enjoyed wide freedom of speech, expression, information, and travel throughout the Yeltsin period. An extraordinary diversity of views developed in the national media. Yeltsin showed himself to be remarkably tolerant of criticism and press freedom. Like other freedoms, this could be, and was, abused by the owners of the main national television channels, Berezovsky and Gusinsky, in the quest for Yeltsin's reelection.

Yeltsin also gave freedom to the regions—to the 89 "subjects of the Federation." In 1990 he had famously invited the non-Russian ethnic republics to take as much power as they could swallow. In the early 1990s, he had studied the model of the German *Länder;* had enacted the Federal Treaty; and had permitted republics and regions to negotiate treaties dividing power with Moscow. In 1995 he took the important step of instituting the direct election of governors instead of appoint-

> In contrast to Europe, Russian power is not the central problem in East Asia. Indeed, the potential gains from engaging Russia in this region—in relations with China, in managing a crisis on the Korean peninsula, in providing energy and other natural resources for a dynamic regional economy rich in other factors . . .—are sometimes overlooked.
>
> —Joint Note
> *Engaging Russia*
> Report to the Trilateral Commission, 1995

ment by the president. He spoke emphatically of his belief in federalism. The results were mixed and illustrated the difficulty and dangers of introducing democratic structures. His policy defused separatist and secessionist pressures, and there were benefits in lifting the deadening weight of centralized control. However, an increasingly chaotic situation developed as regions made their own laws and rules. Many regions were grossly misgoverned by strongmen who abused their independence and their powers, profiting (once they had secured election) from an absence of legal or democratic constraints. The governors dominated the regional legislatures, judiciary, and law-enforcement agencies. Not a few appeared to have links to organized crime.

The economy was the unhappiest part of Yeltsin's second-term legacy. Its dominant characteristics were mismanagement by government and unbridled opportunism in business. The 1995 Trilateral Commission report observed that the new class of businesspeople, including the mafia, whose grip on commercial life was increasing to a dangerous extent, was driven by the desire to become rich and powerful: "[T]he question is whether these narrow motives can be mobilised for the wider good, as they are in mature capitalist systems."

The answer, so far as Yeltsin's second term was concerned, was firmly in the negative. A bankrupt government was manipulated by a small group of businesspeople in their own interests. The economy was dominated by conglomerates assembled through the loans-for-shares privatizations. The larger companies ran private armies and used muscle as a standard competitive tool. Russia became notorious for contract killings. The legal and tax systems were riddled with loopholes and contradictions. Law enforcement was impotent in the face of powerful businesses, or in hock to them. Tax collection was extremely low, and the government failed to put in place the measures necessary to increase it. Wages in the state sector (as well as in nonviable businesses) and pensions were left for long periods in arrears. To try to bridge the gap in its finances, the government borrowed abroad and issued treasury bonds (GKOs) at unsustainable rates of interest.

In August 1998 the bubble finally burst. Having long resisted devaluation, the government defaulted on its debts and devalued. Many banks became insolvent, with huge loss of personal savings. The ruble lost two-thirds of its value. For the second time in the decade, the Russian economy hit bottom. According to official figures, Russian GDP contracted under Yeltsin's rule by some 40 percent.

As Russia's internal situation deteriorated, its standing in the world inevitably declined in parallel. Russia and the West had fallen into a post–Cold War embrace in the early 1990s. The language of partnership was born. Foreign Minister Andrei Kozyrev, though viewed with suspicion at home and in his own ministry, was treated as a friend and colleague by his Western counterparts. Multilateral agencies and Trilateral governments strained to support the transition to a market economy and, they hoped, democracy.

The mood began to change in 1994–95. There were a number of proximate causes: the Russian offensive in Chechnya beginning in late 1994; the looming specter of the enlargement of NATO; and the Bosnian conflict, in which the interests and emotions of Russia and the West lay on opposite sides. The Russian government complained that it was being ignored, taken for granted, or subjected by the International Monetary Fund (IMF) to unreasonable conditions. Western governments entertained rising doubts about Russia's course. These were reinforced when Kozyrev was replaced as foreign minister in January 1996 by Primakov—seen abroad as the embodiment of an older, Soviet view of the world.

By the time of Yeltsin's reelection in July 1996, a pattern had been set for a less cooperative and pricklier relationship between Russia and its main Western and Group of Seven (G-7) partners. It was not an adversarial relationship, but expectations on both sides had fallen. The

G-7 and others continued initiatives to assist economic restructuring. In May 1997, after prolonged and difficult negotiations, Russia and NATO signed the Founding Act, which was intended to open a new chapter of partnership between them. A year later, President Yeltsin was welcomed into the club of an enlarged "political" G-8. This was a further signal of support, despite his mounting difficulties. Beginning in the autumn of 1998, relations came under strain again with the unfolding of the Kosovo crisis, leading to North Atlantic Treaty Organization (NATO) air strikes against Yugoslavia the following spring. Although President Yeltsin's special envoy, Viktor Chernomyrdin, played a key role in persuading Slobodan Milosevic to accept NATO's terms for ending the conflict, NATO's operation had caused deep anger in Russia as well as fears that this could become a precedent for the use of NATO forces in conflicts much closer to Russia's borders. The new Russia-NATO relationship described in the Founding Act was consigned to cold storage. As Yeltsin reached the end of his term, his up-and-down relationship with Western partners was in one of its difficult phases.

Legacy of the Yeltsin Years

In his magisterial biography of Yeltsin, Leon Aron proffers a verdict of one sentence:

> He made irreversible the collapse of Soviet totalitarian communism, dissolved the Russian empire, ended state ownership of the economy—and held together and rebuilt his country while it coped with new reality and losses.[3]

The state continued to own large parts of the economy. A great deal of privatization took place under Yeltsin, but in a way that left much of the economy, including the most valuable hydrocarbon and mineral assets as well as mammoth industrial conglomerates, in the hands of a very small number of people. Corruption and criminality flourished, and market economics acquired a bad name among ordinary citizens

Russia held together in this period, but loosely, owing more to a centuries-long spirit of national cohesion than to effective governance.

---

3 Leon Aron, Yeltsin. *A Revolutionary Life* (New York: St. Martin's Press, 2000).

Much of the country continued to crumble—including its health system. Behind the façade of a handful of grandiose projects designed to boost national pride, such as the rebuilding of the Cathedral of Christ the Savior and the refurbishment of the state rooms in the Kremlin Palace, investment in infrastructure was pitiful.

Leon Aron's verdict rightly omits mention of democracy. Putin has frequently been accused of reversing the process of democratization under Yeltsin. This is not accurate. Yeltsin gave Russians personal freedom—in some cases too much, because this was not freedom under the law, but freedom outside and beyond law, open to exploitation by the strong, the ruthless, and the opportunistic. He spoke the language of democracy: but he did not rule by it or implant it. To the man and woman in the street, by 2000 "democracy" had come to be associated with a sequence of acutely painful experiences: the collapse of the superpower in which they had taken pride, the trauma of shock therapy and hyperinflation, the shelling of the White House, theft through pyramid schemes and corruption, the accumulation of vast wealth by the few at the expense of the many, the economic collapse of 1998 that wiped out savings, and two wars in Chechnya.

This may not be a just verdict on Yeltsin's rule, but it helps to explain his deep unpopularity at the end. In the circumstances of Russia in the 1990s, it would have been totally unrealistic to expect any leader to entrench democracy in a single decade, but it might have been possible to set the country on a course toward a democratic and law-based society. Yeltsin started in one direction, but he changed course in 1993–94, reverting to a traditional model of Kremlin rule. His reign began with euphoria and ended with the bathos of his apologetic resignation broadcast.

Vladimir Putin was bequeathed a country in disarray internally and enjoying little respect abroad.

3

Rebuilding the State 2000–03

> Russia was and will remain a great power . . . The public wishes to see the appropriate restoration of the guiding and regulating role of the state, proceeding from the traditions and present condition of the country.
>
> —Vladimir V. Putin
> "Russia at the Turn of the Millennium"
> December 29, 1999

This chapter reviews President Putin's objectives and how they were advanced until near the end of his first term. Chapter 4 will look at the marked change of direction from the middle of 2003 onward and assess the state of Russia today, in the summer of 2006. These two chapters focus principally on developments within Russia: the three following chapters will look at aspects of Russia's external relations.

The President's Objectives

Putin's "Millennium Statement," issued on December 29, 1999, when he (though not the country) knew he was about to assume the acting presidency, was the only manifesto he put out before his formal election on March 26, 2000. On July 8, he made his first annual address to the Federal Assembly. In these two statements he laid out a set of principles and objectives.

In the statement of December 29, 1999, these included:

- **Rejection of the Soviet command economy and justification of the reforms of the 1990s.** "The current difficult economic and social situation in the country is the price that we have to pay for the economy we inherited from the Soviet Union . . . Today we are reaping the bitter fruit, both material and intellectual, of past decades . . . Russia is completing the first, transition stage of economic and political reforms. Despite problems and mistakes, we have entered the main highway of human development." Putin described Communism as a futile social experiment for which Russia had paid an outrageous price: "[F]or nearly seven decades we were moving along a blind alley, far from the mainstream of civilization."

- **Evolutionary reform and political stability.** "Russia has reached its limit for political and socioeconomic upheavals, cataclysms and radical reforms." It needed a strategy for revival and prosperity implemented by "evolutionary, gradual and prudent methods" and "on the basis of political stability."
- **A Russian model of transformation, not one mechanically copied from the experience of other nations.** "Every country, Russia included, has to find its own path of renewal . . . Our future depends on combining the universal principles of the market economy and democracy with Russian realities."
- **A civic consensus on values.** This should combine supranational universal values—freedom of expression and travel, fundamental political rights and liberties, property ownership, free enterprise, for example—with traditional Russian values. The latter were defined as:
  - **Patriotism.**
  - ***Derzhavnost'* (literally, holding power).** "Russia was and will remain a great power." This had determined Russian mentality and policy throughout history, but a country's might was now measured more by technology, prosperity, and security than by military strength.
  - ***Gosudarstvennost'* (statism).** Russia was unlike the United States or the United Kingdom. For Russians, a strong state was "the source and guarantee of order, and the initiator and the main driving force of change." This did not mean a totalitarian state. Russians had "come to value the benefits of democracy, a law-based state, and personal and political freedom," but they wanted to see the "restoration of the guiding and regulating role of the state."

    - **Social solidarity.**

- **A democratic state.** Dictatorships were transient. Only democratic systems were lasting. Russia needed a strong "democratic, law-based, workable federal state." Experience showed that "the main threat to human rights and freedoms, to democracy as such, arises from the executive authority." Society needed "control over the executive to preclude arbitrariness and the abuse of office." Putin accordingly promised to make it a priority to build up civil society and to wage "an active and merciless struggle against corruption."
- **A long-term development strategy with deeper state involvement in social and economic processes.** Russia needed to create an attractive investment climate and a diversified economy, integrating into world economic structures. Priority should be given to new knowledge and technologies. Putin also promised to tackle poverty, health care, and education.

In his first address as elected president, in July 2000, Putin amplified these themes. He again emphasized the importance of strengthening the state: "[O]nly a strong or effective . . . state is capable of protecting civil, political and economic freedoms," but the strong state had also to be democratic. It needed stronger political parties that had mass support and stable authority—not "parties of officials which are attached to the government."

Four points are particularly worth noting:

- **"Dictatorship of the law."** The law should dictate and limit the powers of the state—to prevent corruption and the abuse of the power vacuum by "shadowy" corporations and clans. Russia needed "a truly independent legal system and an effective system of law-enforcement bodies."
- **A "vertical" of executive power.** This was needed to impose federal authority on the regions and prevent disintegration of the state.
- **The media.** Russian democracy could not survive without "truly free media." This required freedom not only from government interference but also from the commercial and political interests of owners and sponsors, who sometimes even used the media as "a means of fighting the state.
- **The state's relations with business.** Putin said that the state should concentrate on creating a common economic space for the

country, implementation of the law, and protection of property rights. The main obstacles to economic growth were "high taxes, corruption among officials and extensive crime." The state should not increase its role in individual industries or support selected enterprises and market participants.

The need for a stronger state and more effective federal control of the regions was a recurring theme in Putin's subsequent annual addresses, as was the objective of combating corruption. In 2001 and 2002, Putin placed a strong emphasis on the need for reform of the administrative and judicial systems, of natural monopolies, and of the financial and housing sectors. In 2002 he called for military reform and the formation of a professional army; and in the following year he set a deadline for this to happen by 2007. In 2003, the three most important tasks were defined as doubling GDP within a decade, overcoming poverty, and modernizing the armed forces. The growth target was restated in even more ambitious terms the following year—to double per capita GDP by 2010 (that is, within six years).

First Term: Balancing Order, Governability, Reform, and Democracy

The country whose leadership Vladimir Putin assumed on January 1, 2000, was at a very low ebb. As he pointed out, GDP had nearly halved in the 1990s; GDP per head was one-fifth of the G-7 average; average per capita income was less than half the world average; and gross national product (GNP) was one-fifth that of China (the ratio had been almost the reverse a generation previously). It was estimated that Russia would need 15 years of annual GDP growth at 8 percent to reach the per capita level of Portugal in 2000. Against this somber background, Putin was promising to rebuild a strong state in a law-based, democratic form and to establish a properly regulated, modernized, competitive market economy, integrating with the world economic system. Most important, the new president promised stability.

Putin in effect found himself attempting to ride two horses at once—never an easy act. The Russian people yearned for tranquility after a bellyful of so-called reform and democracy in the 1990s. There were millions of Russians content to work in and benefit from the market economy but to whom the concept of market economics was anathema. On the other hand, Putin and his advisers knew that restructuring was essential if Russia was to achieve the goals he had set and fulfill its potential to rank among the world's advanced nations. A report by Sergei Karaganov's Council on Foreign and Defense Policy stated: "[I]f the ruling class does not find in itself the strength to lead society toward a change of power and model of development, then Russia is doomed to decay and destruction."[1] Putin had to find a balance between order and governability (so lacking in the Yeltsin era) and freedom and democracy. He promised both.

Initial expectations among the elite that the new president could manage this balancing act were low. He was seen not as a strong leader but as an apparatchik with little personal clout or experience of economic management who had been installed mainly to be a reliable protector of the interests of the Yeltsin circle (or "family"). These were expectations that Putin was to confound, in various ways, during a remarkably successful first three years in office.

Leadership

From the outset, Putin surprised observers with his hitherto unsuspected political skills (unsuspected even by himself, according to his own account: he had never run for office and found the process distasteful). He came across to the Russian electorate as youthful, fit, sober, articulate, intelligent, hard working, soft spoken, lacking in bombast and empathetic: someone who listened and showed concern for the problems of ordinary people. All of this was in sharp contrast to Yeltsin in his declining years. Putin took the trouble, especially in his first two years, to travel across Russia and touch different constituencies: mothers, farmers, industrial workers, the Orthodox Church, veterans, and the military (one of the largest of all constituencies). At a later stage, he held annual phone-ins and televised mass press conferences, fielding questions from around the country on everything from geopolitics to the dacha gardens, where ordinary Russians still grow most of the nation's vegetables. Putin connected with the people in a way that the liberal reformers had never managed, and he became genuinely popular, with opinion-poll ratings shooting close to 80 percent (Yeltsin's had long been in single digits).

---

1 "A Strategy for Russia—Agenda for the President, 2000" (Moscow: Council on Foreign and Defense Policy).

This personal popularity became one of Putin's two greatest assets. Although it inevitably declined over time, opinion polls five years later still gave him popularity ratings that a Western leader would envy and that far exceeded those of any other Russian public figure.

Administration: A Balance of Factions

Putin's other main point of leverage was his office. The combination of Yeltsin's superpresidential 1993 constitution and of a centuries-old tradition of deference to the ruler puts enormous power in the hands of whoever sits in the Kremlin. For the most part, Putin used that power cautiously and cannily in his first three years. He made himself accessible and took advice from a wide range of Russians as well as a number of foreign sources. The team that he put together in the presidential administration and the government was a carefully balanced coalition of different factions and points of view. Many of the key officeholders under Yeltsin were retained, including Kasyanov (promoted from finance minister to prime minister) and Voloshin (head of the Presidential Administration). Liberals, mostly from St. Petersburg, came into the government as finance minister (Kudrin) and as minister of economic development and trade (Gref) and were supported by some brilliant young deputy ministers; liberals also came into the Presidential Administration—the lawyers Medvedev and Kozak, and the economist Illarionov. They were to be joined not long after by Ignatiev, who replaced the quirky veteran Gerashchenko as governor of the Central Bank. The liberal economists in the administration linked up with influential like-minded members of the Duma, notably Alexander Zhukov and Mikhail Zadornov, who were to play a critical role in keeping the state budget under control.

On the other side of the spectrum, Putin brought in key allies who shared his KGB background, including Sergei Ivanov (initially as secretary of the Security Council, then as defense minister), Nikolai Patrushev (to head the internal security agency, the FSB), and, in the Presidential Administration, Igor Sechin and Viktor Ivanov. The net result was a patchwork of the old Moscow establishment and incomers from St. Petersburg, technocrats and politicians, liberal modernizers and Soviet-style reactionaries, people favoring closer relations with the West and ingrained cold warriors.

The president was the ringmaster. Voloshin and Kasyanov were responsible for keeping the show on the road. Advocates (not merely advocates in the case of many of the Yeltsin holdovers, but self-interested players) of a market economy ran the economy. *Siloviki,* hard men (senior officeholders with a background in the security organs and military) with no love for democracy or civil rights, stood ready to guard the president's rear and enforce the Kremlin's will.

The new administration brought stability to Russian politics. Parties and blocs supportive of the president were in the majority in the Duma; and the Communists, despite holding one-quarter of the seats, proved to be a limp and complacent pro forma opposition. Past or potential opponents were conciliated. Primakov was made chairman of the Chamber of Commerce. He and Luzhkov were treated with respect. Luzhkov continued to enjoy a free hand in running Moscow, but he stepped back from national politics. A pattern developed whereby soft landings and sinecures were found to keep ousted officeholders and people distrusted by the president—Defense Minister Sergeyev, Interior Minister Rushailo, Primorskiy Krai Governor Nazdratenko, St. Petersburg Governor Yakovlev, to name but four—quietly within the fold of the privileged.

Politics: Order or Democracy?

At all times stabilization took precedence over democracy. This was not without justification. Democracy had not merely become unpopular as a result of the 1990s, but the cover of democracy and the reality of unregulated freedom had been serially abused. By any reckoning, Russia in 2000 needed the reintroduction of some order. Liberal democrats recognized this and were ready to participate in the process—but on the understanding that order would be based on due process of law and on principles of democracy, that it would lead to the fuller development of the market economy and free enterprise, and that the long-term goal would be to build a democratic system. Yabloko leader Yavlinsky, for example, made clear that he would support Putin on this basis. So did the Union of Right Forces under Chubais and Nemtsov. So did the two most respected gurus of liberal economics, Yevgeniy Yasin and Yegor Gaidar. But the balance between order and democracy was to become a more and more difficult issue during Putin's first term. Indeed, it was the defining issue of Russian politics—and the definition was to become clear by the end of the first term.

In the political arena, it transpired that democracy, per se, was not a core belief or prime objective within the Kremlin. The president introduced the term of "managed" or "guided" democracy. One of his aides, Vladislav Surkov, was seen to be stage-managing democracy with demonic energy and Machiavellian cunning. Instead of the control by society over the executive of which Putin had spoken, the executive sought tighter control over civil society. Its aim was to orchestrate non-governmental organizations (NGOs) and political movements under the Kremlin's baton. The Kremlin organized a forum of NGOs and invented a pro-Kremlin youth movement. Putin had called for strong political parties—not parties of officials attached to the government—but "managed democracy" produced the opposite.

Putin showed a lawyer's respect for constitutional propriety. He did not govern by presidential edict, as Yeltsin had done for periods; instead he put legislation through the Duma. The Duma at first was not just a rubber stamp. Deputies could, and did, reshape or block legislation—sometimes for respectable reasons, sometimes less reputably because they were in hock to commercial interests (every tycoon had heavies in the Duma, and Duma seats became highly profitable for many parliamentarians). In response, the Kremlin built up its own bloc of "placemen"—labeled "Unity," subsequently "United Russia"—and used the levers of power to manipulate and manage supposedly independent parties such as the Communists and Zhirinovsky's LDPR.

Party management and political skullduggery is not a game unique to Russia. There was a need to ensure both that the government's proper business was not blocked (as had happened in the early 1990s) and that democracy was not hijacked by populist extremists. Nevertheless, the net effect was that Russia moved away from, rather than toward, the evolution of a genuine multiparty system, and the ability of Duma deputies to operate independently declined by degrees.

Controlling the Barons and the Media

Stabilization and the restoration of order had to extend, as Putin had indicated, beyond official politics and into business, the media, and the regions (the so-called subjects of the Federation). In each of these areas there was an objective need for action.

Under Yeltsin, over-mighty tycoons had enriched themselves at the expense of the state, entrenched their competing interests at the heart of federal and regional centers of power, and manipulated the electorate by controlling much of television and the print media. Putin offered a tacit deal. He would not revisit the 1990s, overturn the privatization of state assets, or renationalize. In return, the businesspeople should stay out of politics and the affairs of the state and should play by the rules. The government would establish a level playing field for competing businesses, without the privileges and tax breaks that some had enjoyed at the expense of others, and it would maintain equidistance between them. The days in which business could dictate to government were over.

Driving the message home, the Kremlin destroyed the power of the two mightiest media barons. Television stations controlled by Berezovsky and Gusinsky had played the critical role in Yeltsin's re-election in 1996. Berezovsky had been instrumental in levering Putin into power, creating the Unity party and torpedoing Luzhkov and Primakov as rivals for power. Putin clearly did not wish to allow Berezovsky to maintain a hold over him, and Gusinsky's NTV had become tiresomely critical, satirizing the president and attacking the conduct of the war in Chechnya. Gusinsky was arrested in June 2000 and ordered to surrender his media interests. By April 2001, his independent television station, NTV, had been taken over by state-owned Gazprom, and Gusinsky was in exile. Feeling a chill breeze from the Kremlin, Berezovsky set up an opposition party, Liberal Russia, and resigned from the Duma in July 2000. After his behavior in the 1990s, he was deeply distrusted on all sides, and he failed to attract support. He was forced to sell his 49 percent stake in the national television channel, ORT, although he retained ownership of several newspapers, including *Kommersant,* and, lamented by very few, he took his opposition into exile in London in November 2000.

The ouster of Gusinsky and Berezovsky sent a powerful signal that the Kremlin would not tolerate serious opposition from magnates in the political arena (magnates who used the media, as Putin put it a month after Gusinsky's arrest, as "a means of mass disinformation, a means of fighting the state"). The methods used were crude, selective, and of highly questionable legality. Nevertheless, the forcible removal of two media barons of murky repute (especially so in Berezovsky's case) did not have to constitute, per se, limitation of the freedom of the press.

The Kremlin had the option of establishing a transparent framework of law and regulation (as exists in other countries) within which independent media could operate and give voice, fairly, to different points of view. This was not the course it chose. The Kremlin pressed on through Putin's first term and into his second term with the incremental constriction of the political freedom of the mass media. The national television channels were brought firmly under control. Independent commentators were forced out. An attempt to set up a new independent TV station was crushed. Television editors were given direct, regular instructions by the Kremlin on what—and what not—to cover (any critical coverage of Chechnya was forbidden). Some politicians were allowed on air, others not. The newspapers were not formally censored, but, for most, self-censorship became the order of the day. For appearance's sake, not all outlets were brought into line: the liberal radio station, Ekho Moskvy, continued to be tolerated, as did small-circulation newspapers such as *Novaya Gazeta* and the business paper, *Vedomosti.* Rather surprisingly, the Berezovsky-owned *Kommersant* survived and bore his thumbprint in its attacks on the Kremlin. But the media for the masses were largely under control.

The Vertical: Reestablishing Control over the Regions

Where disobedient media posed a challenge to the group in power, unruly regions represented a more fundamental challenge to the governability and cohesion of the country. Yeltsin had decentralized without clearly establishing federal authority or the demarcation of powers. The regions had taken advantage of the weakness of central government. The result was chaotic. According to Professor Richard Sakwa,[2] at least 50 of the 89 local constitutions and charters contradicted the federal one, while one-third of local legislation violated federal legislation. An examination by the Justice Ministry of 44,000 regional legal acts found that nearly half did not conform to the constitution or federal legislation.

Yeltsin had instituted the direct election of regional governors, but this had not made the regions into beacons of democracy. A few regions were run well and democratically (Novgorod being a shining example); most were not. Sorting out this mess and rebalancing power between the federal center and the subjects of the Federation was one of Putin's first objectives. He was widely supported, not least by those in the regions subject to the worst abuse of local power.

The president applied a combination of constitutional, legal, and administrative measures. Regional governments were ordered to bring

---

2 Richard Sakwa, *Putin: Russia's Choice* (London: Routledge, 2004).

their laws into line with the federal constitution. The Constitutional Court ruled that declarations of sovereignty adopted by many republics were unconstitutional and that the regions did not have the right to set up their own courts. By a decree enacted six weeks after his inauguration, Putin set up seven federal districts to cover the country, each under the charge of a powerful presidential representative (with the rank of deputy prime minister and reporting directly to the Kremlin). Governors were deprived of their seats in the Federation Council, the upper house of the legislature, and some budgets were rebalanced.

The net effect was at least partially successful. The presidential representatives exercised a degree of downward pressure on governors, and legal anomalies and interregional barriers were removed. Governors showed slightly more deference to the Kremlin's wishes, especially when they were short of funds or needed electoral support, but their power and patronage within their regions was not greatly diminished. The Kremlin backed down on measures that would have limited governors to two terms. It effected the removal of the governor of one of the most notoriously criminalized regions, Primorskiy Krai, only to see him replaced by a close associate. In a number of elections, its favored candidate was defeated.

Chechnya: A Failure of Control

Chechnya, of course, fell into a category of its own: the biggest test of the Kremlin's ability to impose order, and its biggest failure. A critical period occurred in the spring of 2000. Russian forces had captured Grozny and occupied the northern lowlands of Chechnya. On the separatist side, Aslan Maskhadov, elected president of the republic for a five-year term, retained a degree of authority, if not full control over the rebel fighters. The Russian leadership spurned whatever chance may have existed of a negotiated settlement with Maskhadov and chose to press on with the campaign—seeking to eradicate hardened guerrilla fighters at home in their mountain terrain, using ill-equipped, poorly coordinated conventional forces not trained for the task.

Six years later, the task has not been completed. In his April 2001 address, the president announced that "having fulfilled its main missions, the army is withdrawing." It didn't. In November 2001, feelers about negotiation led to a meeting at a Moscow airport between Maskhadov's emissary, Ahmed Zakayev, and the then presidential representative for the Southern Federal District, General Kazantsev. The deal offered by Zakayev, which would have kept Chechnya in the Federation, was not pursued.

In April 2002, Putin declared that "the military stage of the conflict can be considered to be completed." Nevertheless Russian security forces in the thousands remained in Chechnya, officially engaged in "mopping-up operations." Chechen extremists continued to take a heavy toll, including in the attacks on the Dubrovka Theatre in Moscow in October 2002 and on government headquarters in Grozny in December.

In 2003, the Kremlin moved toward a policy of "Chechenization." A constitution was approved in March 2003 in a referendum that fulfilled no normal democratic criteria and produced 96 percent approval on an alleged 89 percent turnout. In the presidential election in October, Ahmad Kadyrov was elected with a notional 82 percent after his two most credible challengers had been persuaded by the Kremlin to step out of the race. Kadyrov was a clan leader who had declared jihad against the Russians in 1995. He brought with him a private militia of former guerrillas. After his assassination in May 2004, he was succeeded by an associate, Alkhanov, who is expected soon to be displaced by Kadyrov's notorious son, Ramzan.

What has been the net result of six and a half years of conflict? Terrorism has not been eradicated, as a series of hideous attacks has shown, including the bombing of trains and aircraft, the raid on Nazran (Ingushetia) in June 2004, the appalling attack in September 2004 on a school at Beslan (North Ossetia), and the attack on Nalchik (Kabardino-Balkaria). Russian forces have fought a vengeful war incompetently and with gross abuses of human rights—few of which have been punished—on all sides. Casualties are now numbered in many thousands. To some, the war has proved highly profitable, with streams of federal funding reported to have been diverted into the pockets and dachas of officials and military commanders. Little has been done to win the hearts and minds of the population or reconstruct their lives, and local control has now been delegated to a thuggish clan.

The Economy: A Success for Liberalism

If Chechnya was the biggest failure, the most striking success was in the economy and the reform program.

Along with restoring stability and the state, Putin had placed the development of the market economy in Russia at the top of his priorities. He had promised the reform-weary populace that there would be no more shock therapy, but equally he had nailed his colors to the mast of evolutionary modernization. Even before assuming the acting presidency, he had tasked a team of liberal economists at the Center for Strategic Development, under German Gref's leadership, with production of a long-term reform strategy. Gref's program was published at the end of June 2000. It called, inter alia, for accession to the World Trade Organization (WTO), an overhaul of the tax system, and the targeting of social benefits. Debate within the government led to some delay and dilution. Nevertheless, by 2001 Russia was firmly set on the road of economic and structural reform. The president committed himself to this objective in his 2001 annual address. Stabilization of the regions had been the key task for the previous year; now was the time to move ahead with reform—of the judicial system, the bureaucracy, the budget, taxation, customs. He called for new legislation also on property rights, privatization, and land ownership; harmonization with WTO rules; and reform of defense procurement, the natural monopolies, currency regulation, the public health and pensions systems, the labor code, education, and science. Russia needed "bold and carefully prepared decisions" to ensure that stability did not become "bureaucratic stagnation."

This was a highly ambitious program, and many were skeptical that it would be implemented. For the next two years, however, the skeptics were proved wrong. Beginning in July 2001, the Russian government began to implement its "Medium Term Program of Social and Economic Development for 2002–04." This set out principles and a timetable for regulatory reform, with the aims of reducing barriers to growth and creating a favorable environment for entrepreneurship and investment—within a legal and institutional framework that had been conspicuously lacking in the previous decade. Action followed. By the middle of 2003, Russia had acquired new labor, administrative, and land codes (the land code provides for freehold ownership for the first time in Russia's history). The energetic Dmitri Kozak secured adoption of a judicial reform package of 11 laws. Despite opposition from vested interests, negotiations to join the WTO picked up speed—with the end of 2003 seen as a target date for completion. Plans were drawn up and debated for the restructuring of three gigantic, largely state-owned monopolies—UES (the electricity supplier), Gazprom, and Russian Railways—all of which were suffering from chronic underinvestment and inefficiency and that employed among them nearly two million people. The most immediate effect was achieved by tax reform—with new procedures to deal with the unworkability of the previous system and new rates that lowered the corporation tax from 35 percent to 24 percent and set the income tax at a uniform flat rate of 13 percent.

This was heady stuff, achieved by smart and determined people, enjoying the clear backing of the president. Meanwhile, the momentum of reform was matched and facilitated by momentum in the real economy. Russia rebounded quickly from the 1998 crash, helped not only by the benefits of devaluation but by oil prices that more than doubled from a low of $11 per barrel to an average price in 2000–02 in the mid-$20s to, in 2003, nearly $29 (each dollar on the barrel put a billion dollars of extra revenue into the exchequer). Another critical factor was that, after 1998, the Russian government and the central bank adopted what economists have described as a near-flawless policy of macroeconomic stringency. The exchange rate stabilized. Currency reserves grew from a perilous $8.5 billion in 1999 to over $73 billion in 2003. The state's foreign debt was reduced in the same period from $148 to $106 billion, and the foreign debt–GDP ratio decreased from 93 percent to 39 percent. Inflation was pushed down from 36.5 percent in 1999 to 12 percent in 2003, and in 2000 the budget was brought from deficit into surplus—where it has remained for the five years since.

The rebound showed up as a 10 percent rise in GDP in 2000, after a 6.4 percent rise the previous year, against the much reduced baseline of the years up to 1998. Growth then settled at 5.1 percent in 2001 and 4.7 percent in 2002 before rising above 7 percent for the next two years. Improvements began to show at all levels. The number of people estimated to be below the poverty line fell significantly, though still amounting to a quarter of the population in 2002. Wage and pension arrears were greatly reduced, contributing to the popularity of the new president. Indicators of an emerging and increasingly prosperous middle class began to multiply: foreign travel, car ownership, the construction and improvement of private homes, and an accelerating boom in all aspects of retail trade.

The change of atmosphere was also palpable in the world of business. With rising confidence, capital flight (thought to have averaged $50 billion a year in the mid-1990s) fell to $10 billion in 2002. Foreign direct and portfolio investors began to edge back. Corporate behavior, while nowhere near the benchmarks of the developed economies, was on an improving path. A number of sound, well-run, entrepreneurial companies emerged. Some of the larger corporations changed their ways—the star performer being the privately owned oil company, Yukos, whose share price leaped upward as a result of transparency and better governance. Companies, adopting international accounting standards, began to produce respectably audited accounts. The Big Four international auditing firms found that Russia was becoming their most profitable market (one, for example, has multiplied its staff by more than 10 times in five years.). On the back of higher standards, Russian companies started to approach, and be accepted by, Western stock exchanges and capital markets.

Even in the much criticized judicial system, improvements could be seen. Many a case could still be cited where state power (at a central or regional level) or a local baron had triumphed over fair justice, but international law firms found that they could take commercial and tax cases to court and receive what they regarded as fair and expeditious treatment, comparing favorably with other transitional or emerging countries (this was a turnaround since the 1990s, when international law firms had habitually advised clients to avoid the courts altogether).

Of course Russia was a long way from a state of grace. Corruption seemed to have diminished with the change of administration, but it remained a major issue; so, linked to it, was the impediment of a state bureaucracy unchanged in method and mentality, and largely in personnel, since Soviet times. Organized crime and contract killings were still part of the landscape. The infrastructure creaked from neglect. But, all said, it was a time of hope.

4

From Reform to Control 2003–06

> I am very satisfied with what we have done. I remember the end of 1999 and the condition that the state and the economic and social spheres were in. There is a big difference and this is a positive difference. We have strengthened the Federation, we have brought the Chechen Republic back within Russia's constitutional sphere . . . We have significantly lowered the level of unemployment. We have seen an amazing increase in our gold and currency reserves . . . We have significantly increased the population's real incomes, and that is the most important thing.
>
> —President Vladimir V. Putin
> Press conference, January 31, 2006

By the beginning of 2003, the administration could claim significant progress toward the objectives that Putin had set. Russia had stabilized. "Stability" was the first word to come to any Russian's lips when asked to assess the situation. Plenty remained to be done, but the country was more orderly. The worst extremes of feckless politicians, regional bosses, and business leaders had been curbed. The economy was growing. The administration had used this benign environment to promote reform. To the average Russian the "management" or limitation of democracy was not an unreasonable price to pay for stability and prosperity. The main blot on the record was the manifest inability to manage Chechnya and terrorism successfully. (A poll by VTsIOM in January 2003 showed that support for continued military action, as opposed to negotiations, had sunk to 30 percent.)

Russia's standing in the world had risen. It appeared to be on a convergent course with the West, recognized in the establishment of the Russia-NATO Council and the decision to put Russia into the batting order for chairmanship of the G-8. The ultimate cachet was the attendance of more than 40 leaders from East and West, including all G-7 and EU heads of government, at a jamboree at the end of May 2003 to celebrate the 300th anniversary of Putin's home city, St. Petersburg. The period of humiliation was past.

The Putin Administration Makes a Turn

It was expected that some tension would return to the system in the run-up to the December 2003 Duma elections and March 2004 presidential election. The Putin team would not take chances. In the preelection period, they would keep reform out of sight to avoid frightening the horses. Once the president's mandate was renewed, however, many predicted that he would use his position to push through a new raft of structural reforms and accelerate the drive for modernization. However, that was not to be. In both domestic and foreign policy, Russia began to change course from the middle of 2003—and it has not changed back. The president who had feted the world's leaders in May 2003 found himself the target of criticism by G-8 partners at the Sea Island summit just over a year later. A survey of Russian voters in the spring of 2004 found that 55 percent thought that democracy would develop in the president's second term, and 2 percent predicted disorder and anarchy. One year later, only 12 percent believed that democracy was being instituted, and 43 percent felt that disorder and anarchy were increasing.

The second half of 2003 was the time when, within the ruling group, the glittering lure of short-term opportunism—the chance to seize control of wealth and power—triumphed over the long-term modernization of Russia and its closer integration into the world. It was a victory for reactionaries over reformists, for the bureaucracy over the free market and civil society, for the security organs and old-style apparatchiks over liberal westernizers.

The first and most obvious reason for the change was money. With oil at $29 per barrel on average in 2003 and rising through $38 in the following year, Russia was afloat on a sea of black wealth. This undermined the imperative of reform, the credibility of the argument that

Russia must reform or die. Worse than that, much of the wealth was flowing into the hands (and offshore accounts) of those who had acquired assets very cheaply in the 1990s. The temptation to accumulate serious wealth was irresistible for people in power who had missed out on the previous bonanza.

The second reason was that power under the president in the second term was up for grabs. Putin was about to shake off the Yeltsin legacy and acquire a mandate based on his own popularity with the electorate. He and his associates were set on maximizing his authority, which meant control of the Duma and a convincing first-round victory in the presidential elections. The liberals in the administration were vulnerable. The number of so-called *siloviki,* or law enforcers, in key positions had multiplied. The election presented an opportunity to use muscle to deliver victory and then to steer away from liberalism and back toward old-fashioned means of bureaucratic control.

Foreign affairs also played a part in the mood shift. Through the zero-sum prism of the Russian establishment, Putin was generally considered to have given too much away to the West—for example by condoning the implantation of U.S. military bases in Central Asia after September 11 or acquiescing in the enlargement of NATO—and to have received too little in return. Russian politicians had begun to play on historic fears of "encirclement" and redeploy Cold War fantasies about Western plans to weaken Russia and aid her opponents, even Chechen terrorists. As ever, blaming external enemies became a means of diverting attention away from internal failings and of justifying heavy-booted instruments of control. "As our failures mount," wrote Sergei Karaganov in February 2005, "we snarl and blame others, or construct imaginary plans for countering the great powers."[1]

The Yukos affair was both a signal and a catalyst of the changing chemistry of Russia. Mikhail Khodorkovsky had built up the country's best-performing oil company and one that was moving toward Western standards of corporate governance. His behavior in the 1990s, like that of other magnates, did not bear close scrutiny—neither the way he had acquired and defended his assets nor his handling of the creditors of the Menatep group in 1998. He was no angel, but that was not the reason for his downfall.

---

1 Sergei Karaganov, "Russia's Road to Isolation," *Project Syndicate,* February 2005, www.project-syndicate.org/commentary/karaganov10.

Alone among the business barons, Khodorkovsky chose to pit his strength against the Kremlin. He challenged the president in public over a suspicious deal involving a state-owned company. His placemen in the Duma impeded legislation on energy taxes. He did not conceal his political ambition and was seen to be maneuvering to construct in the 2003 elections a powerful bloc of seats in the Duma answerable to him. Added to which, Khodorkovsky was not showing obeisance to the Kremlin in the way he ran his corporation, but instead was planning to build private export pipelines, negotiating a huge merger deal with Sibneft, and discussing the possible sale of a large holding in Yukos to a foreign company. On the sidelines, he had founded the philanthropic Open Russia Foundation, helping education and democratization, doing good for his country and also for his image and influence.

Mikhail Khodorkovsky had become an overmighty subject. He ignored a multitude of warnings. On July 3, 2003, his close friend and partner, Platon Lebedev, was arrested; this was effectively a final warning. Khodorkovsky declined to step back, sell out, leave the country, choose between business and politics, or take whatever options he was offered. The Kremlin also did not blink. The president is known to regard compromise as a sign of weakness. On October 25, 2003, Khodorkovsky, accused of tax evasion, was seized at Novosibirsk airport, flown back to Moscow, and bundled into a mass cell in a remand prison. Khodorkovsky and Lebedev did not go on trial until July 2004. After long-drawn-out proceedings, they were sentenced eleven months later to nine-year prison terms (reduced on appeal to eight years). This will keep Khodorkovsky safely behind bars until near the end of the next presidential term unless he is paroled. No remotely objective observer of the trial believed that the prosecution had made its case, nor, according to poll evidence, did at least half of the Russian public. In breach of laws stating that prisoners should be interned in their own or neighboring regions, Khodorkovsky and Lebedev were dispatched, gulag-style, to remote camps in the Russian Far East.

The affair did not stop with the imprisonment of Khodorkovsky and Lebedev or with the rapid departure from Russia of other major shareholders in Menatep and Yukos. Whether or not it had been part of the original plan, a second Kremlin objective emerged: the destruction of Yukos as a company, and the transfer of its prime assets to Kremlin control. The company was hit by waves of tax demands, which eventually added up to $28 billion. The tax claims for 2001 and 2002 equaled or exceeded the company's total revenues for the year. It was forced to sell its principal oil field, Yuganskneftegas, which, after a phony auction, ended up in the hands of the state-owned company Rosneft—whose chairman, Igor Sechin, happened to be a deputy head of the Presidential Administration (as well as a former KGB officer and long-time associate of the president).

The Yukos affair sent out a series of messages. First, a serious political challenge to the Kremlin would not be tolerated. Lenin's old maxim still applied: "In political conflicts, the goal is not to refute your opponent's argument, but to wipe him from the face of the earth." Second, the elements now in the ascendancy were blithely indifferent to the country's external image, or to conformity with the norms of legal behavior, or to Russia's standing in the markets and investment climate, or to the best long-term interests of the Russian economy (Yukos being Russia's most efficient oil company, Rosneft among the least efficient). Third, previous statements about the reduction of state interference in business, the non-revisitation of the 1990s, respect for property rights, and the leveling of the playing field were inoperative. Khodorkovsky and Yukos had been singled out for selective punishment, for failing to toe the line or pay their dues. Fourth, power in Russia was still about personal control of assets. Fifth, the balance of power within the *nomenklatura* had shifted decisively. Aleksandr Voloshin, holder of the second position in the Kremlin as head of the Presidential Administration, read the writing on the wall and resigned. Prime Minister Mikhail Kasyanov dissented in public and in private and was eventually fired just before the 2004 presidential election.

Yukos was the start of a chain reaction of events and errors that carried Russia ever further from the course of reform:

- **Elections in late 2003 and early 2004.** The Duma election of December 2003 and the March 2004 presidential election were so overcooked by the Kremlin that they were labeled by the Organization for Security and Cooperation in Europe (OSCE) as "free but not fair," failing "to meet many OSCE and Council of Europe commitments for democratic elections," and by Western academics as "the most constrained and least competitive since the Soviet period."[2]

2 Henry E. Hale, Michael McFaul, and Timothy J. Colton, "Putin and the 'Delegative Democracy' Trap Evidence from Russia's 2003–04 Elections," *Post Soviet Affairs* 20, no. 4 (October–December 2004), 285–319.

Overwhelming victories were achieved through control of television, the use by state agencies of what are euphemistically called "administrative resources," and a degree of subterranean maneuver—notably the incursion into the Communist vote of a new populist and nationalist party, Rodina (Motherland), covertly backed by the Kremlin. This produced in the Duma election 222 seats out of 450 for the "party of government," United Russia, plus a further 73 seats between the Kremlin-friendly LDPR (Zhirinovsky) and Rodina. Communist seats were reduced from 114 to 52. On the liberal side, Yabloko was suspiciously deemed to have fallen just below the 5 percent party list threshold and was reduced from 22 seats to a mere 4 constituency members; and the SPS, which had managed an outstandingly inept campaign, plummeted from 29 to 3. After this outcome in the Duma elections, the Communist and Yabloko leaders declined to give credibility to the presidential election by running against the incumbent. Against a field fairly described as Lilliputian, Putin took 72 percent of the vote. The Kremlin's main concern was to persuade (sometimes heavily) voters to turn out for a cosmetic exercise.

- **Reforms.** Administrative reform introduced after the elections paralyzed central decision making for months while it left the bureaucracy reshuffled but unreformed and even less efficient than before. Ministries were subdivided into agencies and services. The number of ministers and deputy ministers fell (taking out some of the most able reformers at the deputy minister level), but the overall effect was to create more bureaucratic combat zones by turning 23 ministries into 72 new federal institutions (14 ministries and 58 agencies). A year later, one of the president's senior advisers, Igor Shuvalov, commented that the new system had not been effective—"manageability has worsened considerably and it has become more difficult to achieve results." The Organization for Economic Cooperation and Development (OECD) noted that the reorganization had "disrupted the work of many government bodies for much of 2004"[3] without achieving either of its aims of increasing efficiency and reducing conflicts of interest.

---

3 *Regulatory Reform in Russia* (Paris: Organization for Economic Cooperation and Development (OECD), 2005).

- **Chechnya and the Beslan massacre.** The assassination of Kadyrov in May 2004 was followed by the Nazran raid in June, the bombing of two airliners flying out of Moscow in August, and the seizure of the Beslan school in September. Beslan cost 330 lives, mostly of innocent civilians, including many children. The federal and regional authorities displayed shocking incompetence and unwillingness to take responsibility. The president lashed out against unspecified foreigners after the act:

  > Some people want to tear from us a juicy piece of pie and others help them. They help in the belief that Russia—as one of the world's major nuclear powers—still represents a threat to someone. Therefore this threat must be removed.

  The attack was subsequently embellished by presidential aide Vladislav Surkov, who accused Western powers of creating cover for terrorists in Russia, with the help of a fifth column of "false liberals and real Nazis."
- **The Orange Revolution in Ukraine.** The Rose Revolution in Georgia that propelled Saakashvili to power at the end of 2003 had been an unpleasant surprise for Moscow. The Orange Revolution in Ukraine a year later was much worse—worse because of Ukraine's huge importance to Russia and, above all, because the Kremlin and the president himself very publicly intervened on the side of the losing candidate, Yanukovich. There was a strong feeling across the political spectrum in Moscow that the president had been poorly advised, the policy had been misjudged, and the outcome was the most serious humiliation for Russia in many years. Nationalists felt that Russia should have intervened more forcibly and effectively; pragmatists considered that the Kremlin's advisers had made a fundamental miscalculation by aligning with a flawed and unpopular candidate; and liberals saw the action as crude, reactionary, and redolent of the past. All concluded that it had been counterproductive, incompetent, and very harmful to Russia's standing and the president's authority.
- **Benefits reform.** Russia was still operating under a social security system inherited from the Soviet Union and structured to provide benefits across broad swaths of the population. The system was failing. The state was not meeting its theoretical obligations.

Help was not reaching those in greatest need, but benefits were being provided in an undiscriminating way to large numbers of people, including the emerging middle class, who did not need them. One of the objectives of the Gref reform program in 2000 had been to move to a more efficient, targeted system of monetized social benefits. Bringing in a new benefits system became, along with administrative restructuring, a flagship for reform in the first year of the president's second term. A complex package of laws was pushed through the Duma in the summer of 2004 to the background of some public protests. The administration failed to give a proper explanation of measures affecting an estimated 40 million people and to prepare effective implementation. Regional administrations were asked to take on more responsibility for the payment of benefits with less money. When the new system came into effect at the beginning of 2005, it triggered the widest popular protests seen against Putin's administration. The Kremlin caved in, backpedaling on the reforms and promising to raise pensions. A necessary reform had turned into a fiasco.

The cumulative effect of this chapter of mistakes was to reduce the authority and popularity of the president. An opinion poll showed that the number ready to vote for Putin had fallen from 68 percent to 42 percent in the year since May 2004. The Kremlin was seen to be in a jittery and insecure mood, fearful of street protests and "colored revolutions," and highly risk averse. This was the death knell for structural reform. The liberals remaining in the government found themselves marginalized.

Russia in Mid-2006

> Money makes the world go round,
> that clinking clanking sound of
> Money, money, money, money, money, money
> Money, money, money, money, money, money."
>
> —*Cabaret*
> lyrics by Fred Ebb

"Money, money, money" is one Russian political scientist's description of his country today. What is the condition and orientation of Russia in the middle of 2006, at the halfway point of the President Putin's second term of office?

Politics and Government

The dominant issue since Putin's reelection has been the "2008 question": in a country that has always been so dependent on its leader, who will be in power for the next term?

The group around the president—an assortment of competing clans and interests might be a more accurate description—has narrowed. The balance of the Presidential Administration and government has changed with the departure of Voloshin (October 2003) and Kasyanov (replaced as prime minister by Fradkov in the spring of 2004) and the reduced influence of leading liberals such as Gref (still in office but a regular critic of his own government) and Kozak (dispatched to the Southern Federal District, which covers the North Caucasus). The dominance of former KGB officers, especially those from St. Petersburg, and of large commercial interests linked to them has become more marked, whether in the state or private sector.

The authority of this group looked shaky after the debacles in Beslan, in Ukraine, and over benefits, but during the past year the group has avoided further disasters and consolidated its grip on power. If nothing happens to disturb this, group members are well placed to organize another large victory for the party of government in the 2007 Duma election and the accession of their preferred candidate in 2008. The main problem they face is in finding agreement among their factions on a credible leader. The constitution bars the president from a third successive term. Putin has said that he will not seek to change it, and he aims to nominate his own successor; but he has also stressed his responsibility to ensure stability in the country. This has led to some speculation that circumstances could arise in which, despite his stated personal preference, he might be prevailed upon to remain at the helm. It would be reasonable to assume that the Kremlin's preference for the succession (whether the continuation of Putin, or one of a number of mooted candidates) will not be clear until the middle of 2007.

The most significant political activity is therefore taking place behind the Kremlin walls, where "sovereign democracy" (that is, democracy played by Russian rules) has supplanted "managed democracy" as the slogan of choice. At other levels, there has been no advance in the development of independent political institutions. The Duma is more compliant and contains fewer authoritative figures than at any point in the past 15 years. Political parties are weaker. Under revised legislation, single-mandate constituencies will cease to exist at the next election, and party lists will have to surmount a threshold of 7 percent rather than 5 percent. This will wipe out the independents and small parties that hold 100 seats in the current Duma of 450.

The requirements for forming parties and entering elections are extremely stringent and are frequently used by the authorities to disqualify parties. The nationalist Rodina party was barred from running in the Moscow Duma election in December 2005, and in March 2006 it was disqualified from elections in seven out of eight regional legislatures (in which it would have been the most serious challenger to United Russia). This happened because its leader, Dmitri Rogozin, had slipped his Kremlin moorings. At the end of March, Rogozin was replaced by a businessman loyal to the Kremlin. It is assumed that Rodina will now be allowed to contest future elections. On the liberal side, Yabloko and the SPS joined forces for the city Duma election in Moscow—their strongest area. Although they crossed the threshold with 11 percent, members of the parties have claimed that their real vote was up to twice this figure—a claim that is impossible to verify.

A pattern has thus developed in which the concept of an independent and lawful loyal opposition is entirely alien. Political activity is either sanctioned by the Kremlin or treated (if it appears to threaten the Kremlin's interests) as a hostile and illegitimate force that has to be crushed. Witness the fate of Khodorkovsky and also the attacks mounted on Kasyanov since he set up in opposition in early 2005 and declared himself a possible presidential candidate for 2008. The prosecutor general's office rapidly opened an investigation into a property deal involving Kasyanov, and the speaker of the Federation Council accused him of being in league with the United States. Kremlin control has extended to the level of youth movements in the form of Nashi (Ours), which promotes an ugly far-Right nationalist ideology. United Russia has now set itself a target of signing up 30 million members. (The Communist Party of the Soviet Union had 22 million out of a population almost twice Russia's).

Instruments of Power

> Our plans do not include handing over the country to the inefficient rule of a corrupted bureaucracy.
>
> —President Vladimir V. Putin
> Annual address, April 25 2005

The "vertical" of power extending down from the Kremlin relies heavily on two instruments: (1) the state bureaucracy at federal and regional levels and (2) the organs of security, notably the internal security service (the FSB, successor to the internal branch of the KGB) but also including the Ministry of the Interior (MVD) and several other agencies. The two overlap. Putin has brought many ex-KGB officers into government; and organizations like the tax enforcement and counternarcotics agencies are largely staffed by former members of the KGB. The armed forces are less of an instrument of power than they were during the time of the Soviet Union, but they remain an important constituency (with over one million men and women in uniform, supported by large numbers of civilians and reservists and applauded by millions of veterans proud to put on their uniforms and medals).

Bureaucracy. The bureaucracy inherited from the Soviet system has successfully resisted reform. Its wages have increased; its numbers and powers have not diminished. The bureaucracy is permeated by corruption that, according to a recent study by the government's Center for Strategic Research, rose sharply in Russia in 2005. Economy Minister Gref has commented that "all experts have said the level of corruption has grown: it is difficult not to agree with this." A Russian NGO, INDEM, estimated in 2005 that over $300 billion was being taken annually from businesses in bribes, and that the average bribe had increased by over 70 percent in five years. Transparency International puts Russia in 126th place out of 159 countries on its corruption index. Reports of corruption range from habitual bribe taking by the police, the customs and tax authorities, and by bureaucrats issuing licenses and permits, through payment for services supposedly provided free by the state (such as education and health care) and through routine extraction of tithes from small businesses up to larceny on an epic scale involving major business deals and assets. Corruption happens at the intersection of government and business. The higher up the scale, the larger the sums, leading in some cases to massive enrichment.

In his annual address of May 10, 2006, President Putin recognized that corrupt and unlawful self-enrichment by people in state positions and in big business had reached unprecedented levels. These people had "pursued their own personal enrichment in a way such as has never been seen before in our country's history, at the expense of the majority of our citizens and in disregard for the norms of law and morality." He warned that:

> . . . be it a businessman with a billion-dollar fortune or a civil servant of any rank, they all must know that the state will not turn a blind eye to their doings if they attempt to gain illegal profit out of creating special relations with each other . . . we have still not yet managed to remove one of the greatest obstacles facing our development, of that corruption.

No close observer of Russia would disagree with the president's words. Remarkably little has been done over the past six years to crack down on corruption or on the perception that official positions at all levels are habitually and with impunity used for self-enrichment. Immediately after the president's address, three FSB generals and a number of customs officials were fired, and several investigations were initiated. The authorities promised that there would be more action to follow. Whether or not in this connection, Prosecutor-General Vladimir Ustinov was fired in June.

State security. The FSB reports directly to the president and is accountable to no other institution. Alone among federal bodies, its regional offices are not under any form of local control but report only to the center. Its size and budget are secret, but its numbers do not appear to have declined significantly, pro rata, since the collapse of the Soviet Union. Despite the FSB's might, it has been conspicuously unsuccessful in combating terrorism, organized crime, and corruption—which raises obvious questions. However, it is making its presence felt in the arenas of business, politics, and civil society much more obtrusively and intrusively than in the 1990s. The FSB is not an organization that has been cleansed of its malodorous past; it is proud of its antecedence through the KGB, NKVD, and OGPU, back to the founding father of the Cheka, "Iron Feliks" Dzerzhinsky. Until it is cleansed, made accountable, and brought within the law, it will stand as a crypto-Soviet, authoritarian barrier to a free society and fair market economy.

A rebellious Russian pop song of the 1980s encapsulated the problem: "Okay, so they let us break dance; okay, so we can be happy sometimes. But still standing behind the column is the man in the thin tie with cement in his eyes."[4]

Armed forces. The armed forces were once an instrument of power, the pride of the nation and the backbone of society, but no longer. They are in need of thoroughgoing reform, so that a modern wealthy Russian state can have a modern army—professional; properly equipped; capable of different roles including tackling low-intensity combat, civil insurgency, and peacekeeping; with an appropriate doctrine; and under civilian control. What has happened thus far has not been reform, but tinkering. The army still relies on conscription and a doctrine of mass mobilization. Most of the conscripts fail to turn up; those who do are often treated brutally and put to work on construction projects (including building dachas for generals) and similar nonmilitary tasks. Demographic patterns threaten an acute shortage of conscripts in the next decade. Efforts to increase the number of professional "contract" soldiers have not proved very successful. Meanwhile much of the equipment is obsolete or inoperable. The head of the Federal Arms Procurement Service recently commented that only 15 new tanks had been delivered between 2000 and 2004 and 17 in 2005. The biggest problem was that funds were "often spent ineffectively, or even simply stolen."

The president appears to be attempting a further effort to kickstart military reform, and he devoted a large part of his 2006 address to the subject. Putin said that "mass defense procurement" had restarted, and he announced a series of steps intended to lead toward more professional, better housed, better paid, and better prepared armed forces, less dependent on conscripts. Further changes were promised in a subsequent announcement by the defense minister, Sergei Ivanov, with the aim of achieving a 70 percent professional army within three years. Time will tell whether this latest initiative can succeed where earlier ones have failed. Of the need, there can be no doubt.

---

4 Lyrics by the rock group, Televizor, are quoted in David E. Hoffman, *The Oligarchs: Wealth and Power in the New Russia* (New York: Public Affairs, 2001).

The North Caucasus

It could be argued that there has been some improvement in Chechnya. The level of casualties is significantly lower than during the full-blown conflict up to 2002, and Chechnya is under local administration of a sort. But this masks three acute problems. First, the Kadyrov clan who have been placed in charge through rigged elections are running Chechnya in a thuggish and corrupt way, unbridled by law, and will not make it a better place. Second, Russian tactics, including the assassination of Maskhadov, have left the insurgency entirely in the hands of the most extreme Islamist elements, led by Shamil Basayev, which have links to the Al Qaeda network. Third, the risk and the occurrence of insurgency elsewhere in the North Caucasus are rising, infected by Chechnya but not invariably stemming from there. The region is a cauldron of ethnic and clan animosity. Governance is corrupt, unemployment is high, and Chechnya has created a large and floating refugee population. The Russian government has neither proper control nor a strategy. In a closed Duma hearing last October, Deputy Prime Minister Zhukov was reported to have said that Russia did not have an economic or social policy in the North Caucasus or an ideology to counter religious extremism.

The Regions

Following Beslan, the president announced a proposal (since enacted) to abolish the direct election of regional governors. There was no evident connection with terrorism, but it appeared that Putin was seizing the opportunity to deprive governors of the independent power base given to them by Yeltsin. Under the new procedures, the president nominates a candidate to the regional assembly. In the short term, the change has not made a great difference. Few governors have changed. However, over time the Kremlin will strengthen its control and patronage, at the cost of regional pluralism: it would be heroic to assume that the quality of local administration will improve as a result. Polls have shown that the electorate valued the opportunity to vote for local leaders, even if in many cases the performance of the latter in office has been flawed or corrupt. In his annual address for 2006, the president described as an "improvement" to the political system a new law "giving the party winning the majority in regional elections the right to take part in the process of selecting the regional governor." To most electors, this is rather a long step down from actually being allowed to vote for a candidate.

Law Enforcement and Criminality

Law enforcement is remarkably weak for a country with a vast number of people employed in an array of law enforcement agencies—the Federal Security Service, the Ministry of the Interior, customs, the border guards, the tax police, the railway police, the road traffic police, and the various branches of the "militia." This is in part because, at street level, bribery is endemic and in part because hardened criminals have gained the upper hand (or are operating in league with law enforcement officers). The authorities have failed to get a grip on organized crime. In May 2006, the then prosecutor-general, Vladimir Ustinov, estimated that there were over 400 large organized-crime groups in Russia, involving around 10,000 individuals. He declared this to be a national threat.

The inconsistent example set by the authorities undermines law enforcement. In the upper reaches, especially, the law is applied selectively—and those in power centrally and in the regions regard themselves as above the law (in the tradition of Count Benkendorf, the chief of police to Czar Nicholas I, who argued that "laws are made for underlings, not for their bosses"). The selective use of the prosecutor-general's office has not been confined to the well-known cases of Khodorkovsky, Gusinsky, and Kasyanov, but has become the standard operating procedure. It is remarkable how few cases of corruption have been brought against officials of the current administration (charges were laid against two former ministers of Yeltsin's government). In the commercial arena, tax laws have been applied selectively to punish or put pressure on certain companies and individuals, and state or state-favored companies have been able to obtain judgments against rivals—judgments that defy logic (or contradict numerous judgments in overseas courts).

Information and the Media

Those who compare today's Russia with the Soviet Union are well wide of the mark. A Russian who seeks information has access to a vast range of sources (indeed, if the person can read foreign languages, there is access to as many sources are available in the Trilateral area). The Russian government—unlike the Chinese—does not restrict the Internet, to which an estimated 20 percent of the Russian population now has access (although there has been some debate within official circles about possible curbs). Foreign television and radio stations broadcast into Russia and are carried on cable channels and in some cases rebroadcast on official transmitters. There is a panoply of Russian magazines, newspapers, and television and radio channels. They include outlets that put forward a variety of points of view (from the far Left to the far Right) that are freely critical of the administration.

The problem does not lie, therefore, with the range of information available, nor even with the extent of freedom. It is that, in the most important outlets, especially television channels, the content of news is directed by the Kremlin, access is determined by the Kremlin, and political debate is severely limited and oriented toward themes decided by the authorities. Those in the media who are not under direct orders have become practiced in self-censorship. This is a distinct change from the situation five years ago. The editor of *Izvestiya,* Raf Shakirov, was fired for publishing photographs of the Beslan massacre that the authorities wished to suppress. *Izvestiya* has since been sold to Gazprom.

One by one, the best-known independent broadcasters have disappeared from the screens: Yevgeniy Kiselyov, Savik Shuster, Leonid Parfyonov, Olga Romanova. Romanova was taken off the air at REN TV in November 2005 after broadcasting an item about a fatal road accident involving the defense minister's son. Mikhail Gorbachev said her treatment was "a clarion call that tells us that we have lost the last station which kept even a little independence and objectivity in its coverage." REN TV has since been sold to Kremlin-friendly industrial groups (whose core businesses are steel and oil, not television).

Civil Society

Two recent steps have been taken to keep civil society under official tutelage. The Kremlin has set up a Public Chamber that will hold two sessions a year, with the right only to make recommendations to the government and Duma. The 126 members are not elected but nominated—with the president naming 42, who then select the remainder. The chamber will therefore not be representative or independent and will be toothless—more of a decoration than a democratic institution.

Second, new legislation was introduced early in 2006 to tighten Yeltsin-era laws on the registration and funding of NGOs. The most controversial aspects of the draft law, which would have prevented NGOs from receiving funds from overseas, were dropped, and the measure as adopted is comparable with laws in such countries as France, Finland, and Israel. Concern has centered not so much on the detail of the law as on the motives behind it and the way it will be applied. As a

Russian minister put it to us with commendable frankness, "The devil in Russia is in the implementation." The law appeared to stem from Kremlin nervousness after the Rose and Orange Revolutions in Georgia and Ukraine, in which NGOs had helped to organize public protests, and from pressure from the FSB, the successor to the KGB. In May 2005, the FSB chief, General Patrushev, claimed in the Duma—without any credible evidence—that foreign secret services used NGOs to collect information: "The imperfectness of the legislation and lack of efficient mechanisms for state oversight creates a fertile ground for conducting intelligence operations under the guise of charity and other activities." Duma Speaker Gryzlov made a similar accusation the following January. NGOs fear that, as has happened under separate laws concerning parties and religious organizations, the new law will be used to deny registration to those of whom the authorities disapprove. There are already disquieting indications. Steps have been taken to shut down Khodorkovsky's philanthropic foundation, and the assets of the Russian PEN Centre (a critic of the NGO law) were frozen in March.

Economic Policy

The Russian economy in mid-2006 presents a mixed picture. The outward appearance is of a country growing buoyantly and enjoying the fruits of wealth, but—thanks to sound economic management—without the fragility and instability of the mid-1990s boom that turned to bust in August 1998. Russian has a robustness now, and a cushion against future shocks, which it entirely lacked then.

The headline figures are impressive.[5] Russia is in its eighth year of (in the IMF's words) "robust economic growth." GDP growth of 7.3 percent in 2003 and 7.2 percent in 2004 has slowed slightly to 6.4 percent in 2005 and is projected at 6.2 percent in 2006 and 5.7 percent in 2007.[6] In purchasing power parity terms, GDP per head is now estimated at over $10,000 and could reach $12,000 by 2008. The current

---

5 *Russian Economic Report #12* (Moscow: World Bank, Moscow Office, April 2006); "Russian Federation: 2005 Article IV Consultation—Staff Report; Staff Statement; and Public Information Notice on the Executive Board Discussion," Country Report no. 05/377 (Washington, D.C.: International Monetary Fund, October 2005); *Economic Outlook No. 79* (Paris: Organization for Economic Cooperation and Development (OECD), May 2006); *Economic Survey—Russian Federation 2004* (Paris: OECD, 2004).

6 *Economic Outlook No. 79.*

account surplus rose in 2005 from $57 billion to $84 billion; reserves have risen dramatically from a low point of a mere $8.5 billion in 1999 to $225 billion in April 2006, while sovereign debt has continued to fall—reducing in 2005 from $106 billion to $82 billion. Five years ago, Russian politicians were pressing the West to write off Soviet-era debts and warning that Russia would be crippled by a spike in debt repayment in 2003. Now Finance Minister Kudrin has mooted the possibility of repaying all sovereign debt by the end of 2006.

The largest contributor to these figures has of course been the high price of oil and gas. Nevertheless the Russian government (and the central bank) deserve much credit for maintaining macroeconomic discipline. Federal government spending has been kept under control (at just over 16 percent of GDP in 2004–05, projected to edge up to 17.5 percent in 2006), and the federal budget has been in surplus for six successive years (the 2005 surplus represented 7.5 percent of GDP). Meanwhile the Stabilization Fund has been used to corral and neutralize windfall earnings from record oil prices. The authorities have thereby maintained downward pressure on inflation in a difficult environment. The annual rate of inflation in 2005 was 10.9 percent (against 11.7 percent in 2004); the government is targeting 9 percent in 2006, falling to under 6 percent by 2008.

In business, as in the public accounts, Russia has never had it so good, and businesspeople—both Russian and multinational—have never been so bullish. Russia has been one of the best performing and fastest growing of all the emerging markets. The Russian stock market rose by 83 percent in 2005. Russian companies are queuing to launch initial public offerings (IPOs); around 30 are considering doing so on the London Stock Exchange over the next two years. Russian IPOs in London raised nearly $5 billion in 2005 and could raise over $20 billion in 2006 on current estimates.

The requirements of the capital markets are stimulating a gradual improvement in the governance standards of larger companies (though in some the accumulation of wealth has caused a slackening). In the annual "Transparency and Disclosure Survey" of Standard & Poor's, the transparency rating of the largest Russian companies rose from 34 percent in 2002 to 50 percent in 2005. From their stronger domestic base, Russian groups have been expanding abroad, buying assets and companies in the United States, the European Union (EU), Australia, and Africa as well as in the Commonwealth of Independent States (CIS).

The bid by Severstal to merge with Arcelor to form the world's largest steel company, announced as this report goes to press, is the latest and most spectacular example but will not be the last. The home market is extremely buoyant, notably in a retail sector growing at 10 percent or more annually. Sales of foreign cars grew by over 50 percent in the first half of 2005. The Russian population of around 143 million owns 110 million cellular phones.

> Disinflation will remain difficult. Maintaining fiscal discipline will be critical if the authorities are to rein in inflation while limiting the speed of exchange-rate appreciation. The recent decision to put off consideration of a large cut in indirect taxation until 2009 is thus a welcome development. However, more needs to be done to strengthen the legislative framework governing the stabilisation fund and to insulate not only the budget but the economy as a whole from fluctuations in commodity prices.
>
> —*Economic Outlook No. 79*
> OECD, May 2006

The strong performance of the Russian economy has helped to reverse capital flight. The net private capital outflow in 2005 was zero, against $8 billion in the previous year, over $20 billion annually earlier in the decade, and far higher figures in the 1990s. A substantial increase in foreign direct investment (FDI) occurred in 2005—up by 34 percent on 2004. Russia ranked fourth in total FDI among all emerging markets in 2005, behind only China, Hong Kong, and Mexico. Russia attracted twice as much FDI per head as China.

The business boom has not merely propelled 33 Russians into the *Forbes* list of billionaires and more than 100,000 Russians to millionaire status (both in dollar terms), but has had wider effects beneficial to the country. Although the income disparity between the richest and poor-

> Directors are concerned that, with ample oil revenues, complacency has set in and key structural reforms have come to a virtual halt. They saw the recent weakening in investments and slowdown in economic growth even as oil prices have surged as a sign that high growth may be difficult to sustain over the medium term without a more determined effort to accelerate reforms. In this regard, priority should be given to reforms that could bolster the investment climate, nurture new private enterprises, and promote economic diversification, especially civil service and public administration reforms. Directors observed that the Yukos affair had given rise to concerns about state intervention and heavy-handedness on the part of regulatory and law enforcement agencies. They welcomed attempts by senior officials to reassure investors, but noted that concerns in this regard are likely to linger as long as reforms lag.
>
> —"IMF Executive Board Concludes 2005 Article IV Consultation with the Russian Federation"
> September 21, 2005

est segments is alarmingly wide and a potential source of serious social tension, Russia has not only acquired a substantial middle class but has also made inroads into poverty. At the worst point of the 1990s, well over half of the population was estimated to be living below the poverty datum. The current estimate is close to 15 percent.

Measured in these terms, the economic picture appears extremely rosy. Some strains are inevitable with such rapid change and a tidal surge of dollars. There has been a prolonged and vigorous debate within government around public spending, inflation, and the management of the Stabilization Fund. The fund had grown to $53 billion by the end of 2005, and (on World Bank estimates) could reach double this figure in 2006. Arguments for increased spending from the fund appear so far to have been resisted because of concern about inflationary pressures, but, in the view of the OECD (see the quotation on page 55), more still needs to be done. Another debate has centered around investment of the fund and seems also to have been resolved in favor of the economic liberals, with part of the fund to be invested for future revenue in foreign bonds and eventually in a portfolio of equities.

Sharply contrasting, however, with the benign current environment, there is deep concern among economic analysts and many business leaders about Russia's strategic course, the role of the state, and the growing risk of stagnation and missed opportunities over the medium to long term. In April 2005, the minister of economic development and trade, German Gref, warned that "there is no crisis of ideas, but there is a crisis of governance . . . We have no easy reforms and no popular reforms left. Every reform will be painful." A year later, the president of the Russian Union of Industrialists and Entrepreneurs, Alexander Shokhin, spoke of a long-term risk of the deindustrialization of Russia if the current approach persisted. The IMF's executive board has formally expressed its concern (see the quotation on the preceding page) that "complacency has set in and key structural reforms have come to a virtual halt." The OECD took a similar view in its *Economic Survey—Russian Federation 2004* (see page 58) and more recently has noted "a policy-induced deterioration in the investment climate at a time when capacity constraints were already starting to affect performance . . . A renewed structural reform effort, underpinned by fiscal discipline, could boost investor confidence and contribute to increasing potential output."[7] From a business perspective, the European Round Table of Industrialists (representing leaders of 45 of the largest companies in the EU) has argued that continued insecurity for domestic and foreign entrepreneurs would mean that Russia continued to grow below potential, with seriously adverse consequences (see page 59).

The concern voiced so strongly in a time of plenty by these eminent authorities is clearly not about Russia's current well-being or immediate prospects. No one is forecasting another 1998-style crash. Russia is in much better health than a decade ago. The concern is about the longer term. It is that effective action is no longer being taken to address the huge structural weaknesses and socioeconomic problems ly-

---

7 *Economic Outlook No. 79.*

> Russia has enjoyed five years of robust economic growth since the 1998 financial crisis. Nevertheless, concerns remain about Russia's capacity to sustain high growth over the longer term, especially in view of its heavy dependence on export-oriented resource industries, particularly oil. There are dangers associated with such resource-dependent development, including vulnerability to external shocks, the risk of 'Dutch disease' and the institutional pathologies often associated with heavy reliance on natural resource sectors. The major challenge for Russia over the coming years will therefore be twofold. First, given that growth prospects will continue to depend heavily on resource sectors, the authorities will need to pursue policies that allow the further development of these sectors while acting to mitigate the risks associated with resource-dependent growth. Secondly, in order to facilitate the diversification of the Russian economy over the longer term, and thus to reduce its dependence on resource extraction industries, the authorities will need to pursue a range of structural reforms designed to create an environment conducive to investment in non-resource sectors.
>
> —*Economic Survey—Russian Federation 2004*
> OECD

ing just beneath the glitzy surface of Russia's opulence. In the words of the European Round Table of Industrialists: "Russia has an unprecedented opportunity to strengthen its position as a global economic powerhouse." Russia must address three major policy challenges if it is to meet that opportunity; it must create an environment for a modern economy, maximize its comparative advantage in energy and natural resources, and address its long-standing socioeconomic problems (see the quotation on page 60).

> Should the opportunities available now not be seized, Russia could readily take other paths in its further development. As with the European Union, the worse option for Russia is to do nothing. Continued insecurity for domestic and foreign entrepreneurs would mean that Russia continues to grow below potential. In these circumstances, investment, employment, growth and wealth creation will remain lower than they could otherwise have been Effects may include a continuing reduction in the working-age population and life expectancy and a brain drain of Russia's highly qualified scientists and engineers—all helping to prevent Russia from asserting its potential as a global economic powerhouse. Russia clearly deserves more.
>
> —European Round Table of Industrialists
> *Seizing the Opportunity,* May 2006

Environment for a competitive, diversified modern economy. Russia's trade and current account surpluses mask two weaknesses—overdependence on oil and gas, and faltering domestic production.

Over half of export revenues come from the export of oil and gas (51.5 percent in 2002, rising to 55 percent by 2004 and 61 percent in 2005). Of total FDI, over 40 percent was in the energy industry in 2004 and 30 percent in 2005 (notwithstanding the deterrent effect of the Yukos affair). Because of very high prices, exports are growing rapidly by value, but the rate of growth by volume slowed from 11.9 percent in 2004 to 5.6 percent in 2005. Apart from oil and gas, the other major exports are metals, minerals, and timber. The only large-scale export of high-value-added manufactured goods is in defense equipment: arms exports totaled $6.1 billion in 2005 and are forecast to exceed $7 billion by 2007. In short, Russian exports are still playing to the traditional strengths of the Soviet economy and are exposed to demand for a narrow range of mainly primary products.

> On the surface we look to be keeping to our objectives and have had average economic growth of around seven per cent for the past three years, but I want to stress that if we do not address certain issues, do not improve our basic macroeconomic indicators, do not ensure the necessary level of economic freedom, do not create equal conditions for competition and do not strengthen property rights, we will be unlikely to achieve our stated economic goals within the set deadline.
>
> —President Vladimir V. Putin
> Annual Address to Federal Assembly, May 10, 2006

The Russian domestic marked has changed but is afflicted by "Dutch disease" and struggling to compete with high-quality manufactured imports sucked in by the appreciating petro-ruble and avid consumer demand. Imports grew by over 20 percent in 2005, whereas domestic industrial production rose by 4 percent, slowing from 8.3 percent growth in the previous year. In the important mineral resources extraction sector, growth slowed from 6.8 percent in 2004 to a mere 1.3 percent in 2005. There has been a marked slowdown in tradable goods competing with foreign products (for example machine building declined from over 20 percent growth in 2004 to minus 0.1 percent in 2005), with GDP growth being driven increasingly by nontradable services and goods for the domestic market, such as food and beverages.[8] By contrast, the development of knowledge-based civil companies using Russia's traditional strengths in science and technology and of small and medium-size enterprises in general has been weak. A recent World Bank report has ranked Russia only 11th out of 25 countries in Eastern Europe and Central Asia for its ability to invest productively in research and development, even though Russia has the region's highest ratio of researchers in the working population.

8 For further details, see *Russian Economic Report #12* (Moscow: World Bank, Moscow Office, April 2006).

Dutch disease is accentuating Russia's lack of competitiveness, but it is not the fundamental problem. If the economy is to develop, it needs an environment that will encourage entrepreneurship and attract a much higher level of investment. The lack of investment (in infrastructure, equipment, and training) is showing up in capacity constraints that are set to become increasingly inhibiting. The World Bank notes that "in 2005, fixed capital investment constituted only an estimated 18 per cent of GDP, whereas countries that have sustained rapid growth usually have associated investment rates of 25 per cent or higher." The European Round Table of Industrialists has listed steps that could create the necessary climate (this list is similar to the analyses of many experts inside and outside Russia):

- Modernization of the transport infrastructure,
- Reform of the health and social security systems,
- Modernization of the school and university system,
- Development of a more professional public administration,
- Restructuring to improve the efficiency of existing Russian companies,
- A track record of successful antitrust and merger regulation,
- A simplified, transparent, and predictable tax system, administered in a consistent manner, coupled with reliable property rights and an independent judicial system supporting the clear rule of law,
- Increased economic integration with the rest of the world economy, including WTO membership,
- A growing base of healthy small and medium-sized companies within a reliable legal and regulatory environment, and
- Reduced tolerance for corruption at all levels.[9]

What is disappointing is that, having taken a number of significant steps along this road, Russia has either halted or turned back. The state bureaucracy—through its red tape, corruption, opacity, and inefficiency—stands as a major impediment to business and is a deterrent to foreign investors (see the quotation above). Reform of the bureaucracy has fallen off the agenda (although a fresh campaign to improve performance in the public service sector was announced in June 2006 by

---

9 *Seizing the Opportunity: Taking the EU-Russia Relationship to the Next Level* (Brussels: European Round Table of Industrialists, May 2006).

> One of the most serious barriers to increased investment is corruption. Almost 90 percent of respondents say reducing corruption at all levels is the top measure the Russian government should undertake to improve the investment environment. Seven in 10 investors agree that "decisions of many Russian courts in commercial disputes are very susceptible to financial political and other improper influence." Nearly two-thirds of current investors say their companies are impacted by corruption, while only a third reports no direct impact.
>
> The "hassle-factor" of doing business in Russia appears to be increasing for investors. Administrative barriers, including licensing, permitting and red tape, surpassed corruption as the top investment barrier this year.
>
> —From survey of 155 foreign investors conducted by PBN Company for Foreign Investment Advisory Council, Moscow

Deputy Minister Sharonov). Some improvements have been made to the regulatory, tax, and judicial systems, but the momentum has dissipated, and these systems are not operated in a transparent and nondiscriminatory manner. The playing field for business is anything but level, which militates against both the smaller Russian entrepreneurs and foreign investors. The target date for WTO accession has slipped so often that it has become a vanishing peak.

The most regressive development has been the increased direct intervention of the state in business, weakening the private sector, entrepreneurship, and competitiveness. This has taken different forms, from pressure on some companies and preference for others through to acquisition. State power has been used, or is being threatened, to enforce acquisition or control over a range of companies and assets. This started in the energy sector (which we examine below) but has extended to financial, automotive, airline, aerospace, machine-building, metals, and natural-resources companies. Since 2003, the state's share of industrial output and employment has increased at the expense of the private sector, from under 30 percent to over 40 percent (with an estimated 5 percent transfer in 2005 alone) in a process described by Anders Åslund of the Institute for International Economics as "renationalization . . . driven by the interests of state officials looking to extend their power and wealth."[10] This is not renationalization for reasons of ideology or economic policy. Russian policy makers are well aware, for example, that a competitive gas market and a restructured, privatized Gazprom would deliver much higher performance and revenues to the nation than the existing state-owned monopoly. It is, instead, a matter of accumulating the control of assets in the hands of the group currently in power. Professor Yevgeniy Yasin has spoken of the "higher echelons of bureaucracy" trying "to reclaim some of the influence which they previously had to share with business." One of our other Russian interlocutors was more blunt: this was "the redistribution of property from one group to another under the label of restoring state control." However the process is characterized, a large swath of Russian industry is now under the direct control of Kremlin or government officials, often combining their official duties with chairmanship or membership of company boards, notwithstanding the obvious conflicts of interest. Inefficient companies have been bolstered at the expense of more efficient ones and will become a drain on the public purse. Free-market conditions have been undermined.

Potential of Russia's comparative advantage in energy and natural resources. Energy puts Russia in an enviable position—it has 27 percent of the world's proven gas reserves and 6 percent of oil reserves (Russia is the world's second-largest oil producer, the largest producer outside OPEC, and it also possesses a great deal of exploration potential on land and offshore), huge coal deposits, and hydroelectric and nuclear power. The importance of making the most efficient use of this asset is self-evident. The coal industry was privatized in the 1990s, and has become relatively efficient. Nuclear power, as in many countries remains in state hands and may be expanded in order to release more gas for export. The key questions concern the future of gas and oil: in

---

10 Anders Åslund, "The Folly of Renationalization," *Moscow Times*, May 23, 2006.

> We need to put in place the conditions for more rapid technological modernization in the energy sector. We need to develop modern refining and processing facilities, build up our transport capacity and develop new and promising markets. And in doing all of this we need to ensure both our own internal development needs and fulfil all of our obligations to our traditional partners . . . We must also take action to make our energy consumption radically more efficient.
>
> —President Vladimir V. Putin
> Annual Address to Federal Assembly, May 10, 2006

particular whether state ownership and domination of the industry and the preservation of monopolies will best meet Russia's needs—for investment in exploration and advanced technology, for increased production, for more efficient distribution, for higher environmental standards, and, not least, for the maximum benefit through export earnings and tax and royalty revenues. State ownership is not necessary in order to ensure public control over the nation's vital strategic resources: in Russia, as elsewhere, the state exercises tight control over the industry through legislation, regulation, licensing and taxation. Public ownership is a legitimate model applied in many countries with varying degrees of effectiveness; but the question for Russia is whether the present mix of public and private, national and multinational, participation is working to the country's advantage, now and in the future.

Russia's energy strategy has changed under the current administration. When President Putin took office, plans were formed for the restructuring of Gazprom; and 90 percent of the oil was produced by independent, private sector companies. A number of multinational companies—notably BP in the TNK-BP joint venture, Shell, Exxon, Conoco-Phillips, Total, Norsk Hydro, BASF, and EON—have invested in the market in partnerships with the Russian state and private operators. The private sector has proved successful in developing new re-

> At some point it will probably be necessary for the gas sector to become one of the main drivers of export growth. This makes the restructuring of the state-dominated and largely unreformed gas sector a particularly important priority.
>
> —*Economic Survey—Russian Federation 2004*
> OECD

sources (such as the Sakhalin II project to build Russia's first liquefied natural gas [LNG] export terminal) and in boosting production through investment, better management, and state-of-the-art technology: between 2001 and 2004, the best privately owned companies raised output by over 90 percent, the state-controlled companies by under 20 percent.

Despite this, policy has veered in the direction of enlarging the state sector. The plan to develop a competitive gas market in Russia and to reorganize Gazprom on commercial lines was shelved in 2003, explicitly for political reasons. President Putin described Gazprom then as "a powerful political and economic lever of influence over the rest of the world." Over the past year Gazprom has also acquired an oil company as a subsidiary through the enforced sale to it of Sibneft (whose owners had agreed two years previously to a merger with Yukos).

Gazprom made a bid in 2005 to swallow up the state oil company Rosneft. This was blocked after a sharp battle within the Kremlin (where Gazprom's chairman, Dmitriy Medvedev, and Rosneft's chairman, Igor Sechin, were two of the president's most senior aides). Rosneft instead became the prime beneficiary of the dismemberment of Khodorkovsky's Yukos, acquiring—in highly controversial circumstances over which litigation continues—the Yuganskneftegas oil field. This now accounts for 70 percent of Rosneft's production; from generating 5 percent of Russia's total oil production, Rosneft's share has risen to 16 percent.

Rosneft has declared its intention to become Russia's leading oil producer by 2010 (presumably through further state-assisted acquisitions rather than by organic growth), thereby overtaking the current market leaders, Lukoil and TNK-BP. Gazprom, which produces 85 percent of Russia's gas and has monopoly control of export pipelines, is the world's largest gas producer. Following the lifting of a ring fence on Gazprom's shares, the company's capitalization has risen above $260 billion, making it second only to Exxon among the world's energy giants. Rosneft is planning an IPO of part of its shareholding on the London Stock Exchange in July 2006. As with Gazprom, this will presumably prove beneficial not only to the state—the majority shareholder—but also to company insiders and other minority shareholders. Size, however, does not equate with efficiency. Both Gazprom and Rosneft have high levels of indebtedness, poor track records for investing in production and raising output, and extremely opaque and idiosyncratic governance. The economic benefits to Russia, therefore, of having two very large energy companies under majority state ownership are open to question.

Because the current strategy does not appear to have attracted enough investment into exploration and production and into boosting export capacity through pipelines and ports, doubts have arisen over Russia's ability to raise output of oil and gas in the remainder of this decade. (The International Energy Agency [IEA] estimates that investment up to 2030 of just under $1 trillion will be required to sustain the Russian energy industry.) In 2004, the Ministry of Economic Development and Trade warned that the year-on-year increase in oil production was slowing down and could come to a halt in 2007. Output grew in 2005 by only 2.5 percent, the smallest increase since 1999. The executive director of the IEA, Claude Mandil, commented in April 2006 that expectations for Russian oil supply growth were too optimistic and that the Organization of Petroleum Exporting Countries (OPEC) would need to fill a gap up to 2010. Evidently recognizing the need for higher investment, President Putin has proposed tax incentives for the development of new oil fields in the Arctic and Eastern Siberia; this would help the longer-term prospects but inevitably will take time to show in increased output.

Gas production has also become a problem. We shall consider in later chapters the value of Gazprom to Russia as an instrument of foreign policy. From the economic and commercial standpoint, the key issues are whether the present model of the Russian gas industry is the best way for Russia to use its comparative advantage as the global supplier with the largest reserves and whether Gazprom is performing effectively as a company.

On the first of these points, we face the paradox that, despite its massive reserves, Russia is struggling to produce and transport enough gas to meet its commitments for domestic supply and export, let alone to take advantage of rising global demand and high prices. The industry model is working poorly all the way down the supply chain. In production, Gazprom relies for three-quarters of its output on three giant fields, all of which are in decline. A fourth field, Zapolyarnoye, is expected to peak in 2008 and then decline and is seen by the IEA as the last source of relatively cheap gas in Russia. Total output has barely increased over the past four years, and a leading Russian expert, former deputy energy minister Vladimir Milov, estimates that Russia could face a shortfall of about 1 billion cubic meters of gas by 2010. In transportation, Gazprom controls Russia's 150,000-kilometer pipeline network. Much of this is reported to be in a poor condition and leaking gas because Gazprom has not invested the sums required for maintenance and upgrading.

Meanwhile, Gazprom has used its monopoly control to limit access by independent producers. For lack of pipeline access, independent companies have been unable to market significant reserves and are reduced to flaring associated gas from oil fields, which is wasteful and damaging to the environment. Gazprom has also failed to exploit demand by increasing export capacity. Gazprom has not yet built any facilities for the export of LNG although some are now projected in western Russia, and Gazprom has taken a minority share in the Shell-led Sakhalin LNG project in the Far East. With the aid of tax breaks, the company has built the very expensive Blue Stream pipeline under the Black Sea to Turkey, which is said to be running at only a little over 30 percent capacity, and the company has failed thus far to build any pipelines to China, where potential demand is far higher.

At the distribution and sales end of the chain, the model inherited from the Soviet Union is massively wasteful. Gas is sold to household and industrial users at very low prices (between one-quarter and one-seventh of the prices that can be secured at export), representing a loss to the company and no incentive for conservation and efficient utilization. There is little appreciation that the heat and power thus squandered equate to euro and dollar bills floating out of open windows. The government is raising tariffs incrementally. A rapid price hike to anywhere near export prices would cause huge social and economic disruption and would not be feasible, but what is lacking is a policy oriented toward the eventual creation of a genuine internal market.

The net result is not only an inefficient domestic supply chain, subject to frequent breakdowns, but an apparent shortfall in the ability to meet export commitments. Despite sitting on the world's most abundant reserves, Russia has recently depended on purchases from Turkmenistan, Kazakhstan, and Uzbekistan in order to supply its customers. As the only existing export routes for these three countries lie through Russia, Russia has been able to buy their gas at low prices in order to sell profitably to Western Europe: an effective stranglehold. The extent of the shortfall is in dispute. The IEA has long argued that a significant supply gap is developing in Russia (masked by the transshipment of Central Asian gas). Claude Mandil of the IEA said recently that, according to the IEA's data, "Gazprom will not have in the coming years enough gas to supply even their existing customers and existing contracts." Gazprom rebutted this, claiming that it had the capacity to raise production steeply: "We produce as much gas as is needed by the market," said Gazprom's deputy chief executive officer, Alexander Ananenkov. "There is no gas deficit and there won't be one."

A second, and related, question concerns the structure and performance of Gazprom as a company. This is of great importance to the Russian economy as Gazprom accounts for almost 10 percent of GDP. Gazprom is a huge undertaking, employing 330,000 people. A striking feature of the company is how much of its human and financial resources are deployed, mostly unprofitably, outside its core energy business. Gazprom's activities include banking, a media company, mining equipment, a porcelain factory, agriculture (it is one of the biggest owners of agricultural land in Russia), construction, a soccer team, and a ski resort under development by the Black Sea. Almost 40 percent of Gazprom's employees and $14 billion of its assets are outside the oil and gas business. In 2004 these noncore businesses are estimated to have generated a loss of $350 million.

By any commercial standard, Gazprom is being managed with exceptional inefficiency. Its returns on energy assets are very low. Its market value measured against energy reserves was calculated by the *Financial Times* on March 14, 2006, at $1.30 per barrel of oil equivalent, against around $15 per barrel for major Western companies. In the four years to 2004, according to Vladimir Milov, Gazprom's costs grew twice as fast as its profits. And a company that should be generating huge profits for Russia has been relying on tax breaks from its majority owner, the state. One expert has estimated that Gazprom has been taxed at one-quarter of the energy industry average per barrel of oil and one-sixth of the level of the highest-paying independents.

Clearly some serious questions need to be asked about Gazprom's investment policy. Claude Mandil of the IEA has estimated that "investment in the Russian gas sector needs to be about $11 billion a year if production and export goals are to be met."[11] Instead of focusing on new gas production and infrastructure, however, Gazprom has sunk money into a declining oil producer (Sibneft, at $13 billion), petrochemicals and power companies that need additional investment, as well as into unprofitable projects like Blue Stream and loss-making noncore businesses.

It is hard to avoid the conclusion that the maintenance of Gazprom in its present form represents a massive opportunity cost to Russia. Perhaps the last word should be left to the minister of economic development and trade, German Gref, who sits on Gazprom's board and publicly opposed the company's acquisition of Sibneft. Gref declared in January 2006:

> The ineffectiveness of Gazprom is obvious. You cannot use administrative levers to make such a huge company work more effectively. The market mechanism must be turned on.

Inherited socioeconomic problems, including demographic decline. Since 2000, poverty in Russia has been almost halved. At most levels, Russians have a higher standard of living than ever before, but the country's social systems have not undergone fundamental reform and are therefore based on outdated models that in places are close to collapse. As already noted, this is having a negative effect on the economy. Poor social infrastructure is feeding into a steep decline in population, which threatens to shrink the workforce and become a serious constraint on future economic development. As the President Putin has stressed, this is one of the most acute challenges facing Russia. Russia's newfound wealth, if directed the right way, provides an opportunity to tackle the challenge. It is vital to Russia's modernization but will require a huge and sustained effort.

The Soviet education system produced high levels of literacy, numeracy, and scientific and technical excellence. But it did not generate many of the skills required in the modern economy. With the growth in the economy, capacity constraints are becoming evident in areas such

---

11 *Financial Times,* March 22, 2006.

> What is most important for our country? The Defense Ministry knows what is most important. Indeed, what I want to talk about is love, women, children. I want to talk about the family, about the most acute problem facing our country today—the demographic problem.
>
> —President Vladimir V. Putin
> Annual Address to Federal Assembly, May 10, 2006

as management, information technology, and finance. The education and scientific research system is now underfunded, underequipped, and laboring under outmoded structures and methods. The efforts of an enlightened minister of education and science to introduce reforms have run into dogmatic resistance from the old establishment. Education has been designated as one of four priority national projects and additional funding allocated to it. The direction is clear but implementation is proving difficult.

As noted earlier, the government's attempt in 2005 to introduce a package of reforms to monetize and target social security benefits met a hostile reaction on the streets. In the ensuing retreat, the government committed itself to large increases in state pensions. Russia is left with a muddled and unreformed benefits system and a pension fund in a deficit that is projected to grow. The World Bank has recommended that the Stabilization Fund should be used to capitalize the pension fund and accumulate a reserve to meet the future social needs of the country.[12]

The facts of Russia's demographic crisis are stark. Poor health and low-quality health care play a significant part in it. The Russian population—now estimated at 143 million—has fallen by 5 million since 1993, is falling by 700,000 annually, and is projected to fall by 1 million a year after 2010. Demographers offer a range of projections for the longer term. In its April 2006 report, the World Bank projects a decline

---

12 *Russian Economic Report #12* (Moscow: World Bank, Moscow Office, April 2006).

> In the Russian Federation, female life expectancy (72 years) is close to the level of 1955; male life expectancy (59 years) is three years less than in that year, and is now at the same level as in Eritrea and Papua New Guinea. At present levels of mortality, less than six out of every ten 15-year-old Russian boys can expect to survive to the age of 60, while almost eight out of every ten Brazilian or Turkish boys and nine out of ten British boys can expect to live until 60.
>
> —*Russian Economic Report #12*
> World Bank, 2006

in the order of 17 percent by 2050;[13] but its 2005 report, *Dying Too Young*, expected a decline by over 30 percent during the next 50 years if current trends persist—implying a midcentury Russian population of about 100 million.[14] Experts from the Center for Demography and Human Ecology in Moscow have projected a similar figure unless large-scale immigration occurs.

The consequences will be particularly severe among the working-age population and will begin to be felt within the next few years. Russia has a working-age population of about 87 million, of whom 67 million are officially registered as employed. Based on current trends, the able-bodied population will decline by 18 million over the next 20 years, but economic growth at the current 6–7 percent would create demand for an additional 7 million in the workforce by 2015 alone. The labor market is already getting tight in Moscow and St. Petersburg, especially in certain sectors.

---

13 *Russian Economic Report #12* (Moscow: World Bank, Moscow Office, April 2006).

14 *Dying Too Young: Addressing Premature Mortality and Ill Health Due to Non Communicable Diseases and Injuries in the Russian Federation* (Washington, D.C.: World Bank, 2005).

> Two decades ago, youth aged 0–14 years constituted about one-quarter of Russia's population, and those aged 60 years and above made up 14 percent of the total. Now, those aged 0–14 have dropped to 18 percent . . . [By 2025] the proportion of persons aged 60 and over will increase to more than one-quarter of the Russian population.
>
> —*Dying Too Young*
> World Bank, 2005

What makes population decline more acute in Russia than elsewhere in Europe is not so much the low birth rate as the high death rate. Russia's fertility rate is low but is somewhere near the European average, and it is marginally above Spain's and Italy's. Average life expectancy in Russia, however, is only 65, against an average of 78 in the EU. The big problem is male mortality, which peaked at 65 in the early 1960s and early 1980s but has fallen to 59.

Dying Too Young sets out a range of causes of premature mortality from incidents and noncommunicable diseases:

- Cardiovascular disease (three times the U.S. rate);
- Cancer (well above the EU average);
- Traffic injuries (over 34,000 deaths in 2004, mostly among males of prime working age; the highest road death rate in Europe);
- Suicide (over 59,000 deaths);
- Poisoning (67,000 deaths, mostly from alcohol);
- Homicide (47,000 deaths, mostly alcohol related; one of the highest rates in the world); and
- Cirrhosis of the liver (37,000 deaths).

These figures do not include tuberculosis or HIV/AIDS. About 9,000 Russians have died from AIDS, but over one million are believed to be HIV positive, and the figure continues to rise. Drug use has been primarily responsible for the spread of HIV in Russia. In 2005, 340,000 drug addicts were registered, but the actual number of drug abusers is thought to be five to eight times this number. It is the younger working age and late adolescent population that is most affected by HIV and drug abuse.

In his annual address, President Putin set out a three-pronged approach to the demographic crisis, comprising measures to reduce the death rate (including improved road safety and curbs on bootleg alcohol), an effective immigration policy, and family support programs to increase the birth rate. Inward migration can be no more than a partial solution and would require many obstacles to be overcome. As by far the largest causes of premature deaths are cardiovascular disease and cancer, improving the health of the nation would make a significant difference. The health-care system has been selected for extra funding as one of the four national projects. The World Bank believes that the project should have a positive impact but will not correct the structural weaknesses in the health system. It has argued that more fundamental changes are needed to combat the health crisis and the newer challenges of HIV-AIDS and tuberculosis.

Conclusion

To sum up, Russia in mid-2006 is in some ways a better place than ever before. The country has never been so prosperous, its citizens enjoy a degree of personal freedom that they never experienced before the 1990s, and Russia is making an increasingly important contribution to the global economy. High oil and commodity prices have helped to bring this about, but so have government policies promoting stability, sound macroeconomics, and some important reforms. If the right policies were to be followed (and depending also on the extent of the demographic problem), Russia would have the capacity to become one of the world's major economies over the next two decades. Under the celebrated Goldman Sachs projection of 2003,[15] Russia's GDP in dollars would overtake Italy in 2018, France in 2024, the UK in 2027, and Germany in 2028; and by 2050 GDP per capita would be comparable with that of the Group of Six (G-6) and well ahead of Brazil, India, and China (the other BRICs).

---

15 "Dreaming with BRICs: The Path to 2050," Global Economics Paper no. 99 (New York: Goldman Sachs, October 2003), www.gs.com/insight/research/reports/99.pdf.

This is the glittering opportunity for Russia. But this opportunity will not be taken if the approach and policies of the past three years become not a passing phase in the transition but a long-run trend of bureaucratic state-corporatist stagnation under the control of a small, self-interested, and self-perpetuating group. In the chapters that follow we examine the external and internal consequences.

5

The Big Two and the Big Eight: Russia, the United States, and the G-8

Like its Canadian, European, and Japanese allies, the United States has a compelling strategic interest in seeing Russia evolve into what its own reformers have long called a "normal, modern country," at peace with itself and the world. Such a Russia would be a mature democracy with the institutions necessary for transparent, pluralistic governance; checks and balances; a broad-based civil society; a healthy NGO sector, a diversified, efficient economy; and—crucially—the rule of law.

The American interest in Russia's evolution in this direction is rooted not just in idealistic hopes for the future but in a lesson of history: how Russia treats its neighbors and conducts its foreign policy in general has always tracked closely with how its leaders treat their own people. That makes the nature of Russia's domestic politics relevant to the security of the international community and, therefore, to the security of the United States.

Even under the czars, Russia preyed on the minds of American statesmen for ideological as well as geopolitical reasons. In 1897, a 39-year-old Theodore Roosevelt, then assistant secretary of the navy in the administration of William McKinley, concluded that Americans would never be able to get along with a country that despised "our political institutions." Moreover, the character of Russia's own institutions—the czarist monarchy itself and the secret police—made it a menace to countries on its borders. As long as "the Russian" was allowed to "keep absolutism," wrote Roosevelt, that country would "possess infinite possibilities of menace to his neighbors."[1] In 1901, after Roosevelt had ascended to the presidency, he confided to his associ-

---

1 Edmund Morris, *Theodore Rex* (New York: Random House, 2001), 24–25.

ates and to his diary that he was still brooding about Russian refusal to accept the political norms associated with "civilization."

The challenge posed by the Russian system of rule grew far more acute when it went from being a brittle anachronism to an experiment in Communist dictatorship that claimed to be the wave of the future and to represent the workers of the world. Woodrow Wilson, according to one historian, "regarded the Bolshevik regime as a demonic conspiracy that had destroyed the democratic promise [of post-Tsarist Russia] . . . And he found particularly offensive its doctrine of class warfare, the dictatorship of the proletariat, its suppression of civil liberties, and its hostility toward private property."[2] In 1918, two months after the October Revolution, Wilson promulgated his Fourteen Points partly to counter the appeal of Communism, especially in war-torn Europe. But in doing so, he emphasized help and integration rather than isolation and punishment. Point 6 promised Russia a "sincere welcome, . . . assistance also of every kind [and] intelligent and unselfish sympathy" if it would join "the society of free nations." Rather than throwing down the gauntlet to what would soon become the Soviet state, Wilson was offering an inducement for postrevolutionary Russia to adopt what he saw as a new set of international norms, notably including democracy, as championed by the United States.

The possibility that Russia would ever accept—not to mention meet—that standard never seemed more remote than in the earliest, darkest days of the Cold War. Yet even then, George F. Kennan made the case for combining strategic resolve with patience and optimism in American policy toward the USSR. In an article that Kennan wrote in 1947 for *Foreign Affairs* on "The Sources of Soviet Conduct," he discerned in the USSR "tendencies [that] might eventually find their outlet in either the break-up or the gradual mellowing of Soviet power." Given time, Kennan argued, the Soviets might abandon their pretensions to commanding an armed camp in a divided world and join a single community of nations.

However, four years later, again in an article in *Foreign Affairs,* "America and the Russian Future," Kennan added a note of caution to his advice for those who came after him in designing and executing American policy:

2 Ronald E. Powaski, *The Cold War: The United States and the Soviet Union, 1917-1991* (New York: Oxford University Press, 1998), 8.

> When Soviet power has run its course, or when its personalities and spirit begin to change (for the ultimate outcome could be one or the other), let us not hover nervously over the people who come after, applying litmus papers daily to their political complexions to find out whether they answer to our concept of "democratic." Give them time; let them be Russians; let them work out their internal problems in their own manner. The ways by which people advance toward dignity and enlightenment in government are things that constitute the deepest and most intimate processes of national life. There is nothing less understandable to foreigners, nothing in which foreign interference can do less good.

Kennan lived to see both the mellowing and the breakup of the Soviet system. Yet right up until he died, at the age of 101 in March 2005, he doubted whether the United States could, in any significant and salutary way, influence the internal processes that would determine the next stage of Russia's evolution.

Much of the American deliberation over Russia policy during the past 15 years—and especially since Vladimir Putin began to put his own authoritarian stamp on the country—has revolved around the question of whether the United States should, as Kennan put it, "let" the Russians be Russians, finding their own path to their own future at their own pace; or whether, as others have argued, the United States and its fellow leading democracies should identify what they consider to be the right path and then provide incentives for Russia to find it and stay on it.

That question has been debated inside Republican and Democratic administrations as well as between representatives of the two parties; it has been debated between Americans and Russians; and it has been debated among Russians themselves, some of whom have objected to what they, like Kennan, call "interference," while others have pleaded for the United States to use whatever influence it has with the Kremlin to persuade its principal resident to exorcise the recidivist dictatorial spirit that seems to haunt those premises.

The United States and Russia will both hold presidential elections in 2008. In both cases, the incumbents are constitutionally prohibited from seeking a third term (assuming the constitutions are not amended). The last two years of official interaction with President Putin will be an opportunity for President Bush to refine and clarify U.S. policy at time when Russia's development is still very much in flux. One of several forums for doing so will be the annual summits of the G-8, starting with the one that will be held in St. Petersburg on July 15–17, 2006. The venue is symbolically appropriate: a post-Soviet Russian leader will be convening his counterparts from other major powers in the pre-Soviet Russian capital, built by Peter the Great as a part of an earlier campaign to modernize Russia and open it to the West.

We hope Bush will use both his public statements and his private sessions with Putin, in St. Petersburg and in subsequent encounters, to affirm, unambiguously, the stake that the United States and the world have in the positive trends, which we identify in chapter 2 of this report, eventually prevailing over the negative ones that now seem in the ascendant. For Bush to stress that point would be consistent with the priority he has put on democratization as an overarching objective of his foreign policy. He would also be reestablishing continuity with his 10 predecessors, going back to the president Kennan served so well, Harry Truman.

From Containment to Partnership

During the 1952 presidential campaign, John Foster Dulles, speaking for the Republican Party, floated the idea of "rolling back" Soviet power. But once Dwight Eisenhower was in the White House—and George Kennan had moved to Princeton—the new administration quickly adopted its predecessor's policy known by the single word for which Kennan is best known: containment. It meant blocking further Soviet expansion but leaving the Soviet system in place. It was in that spirit that Eisenhower was cautiously receptive to Khrushchev's professed willingness to make "peaceful coexistence" the basis for U.S.-Soviet relations. Tense and often frigid as those relations were, the United States and its NATO allies still found ways of engaging not just the Soviet leaders in diplomacy but at least some Soviet citizens as well. Over time, the process of exposing them to the outside world—through cultural and trade exhibitions and educational exchanges and, most important, through radio broadcasting—slowly corroded the effectiveness of Soviet propaganda.

The importance of people-to-people programs was underappreciated at the time and, even with the benefit of hindsight, remains so today. That is largely because the U.S.-Soviet standoff was the most dangerous relationship between two countries in history. All eyes were on what was happening between the top men in the White House and the Kremlin. Whether they were scowling at each other from a great distance or shaking hands at a summit, everyone knew that they could start global thermonuclear war. The crises in the early 1960s over Berlin and Cuba dramatized that danger, so it was natural that John F. Kennedy and Nikita Khrushchev would be known as the Big Two. That designation continued with their successors.[3]

However, even during those decades when American and Soviet leaders were concentrating on the task of keeping the Cold War from turning hot, there was a persistent and powerful impulse in the United States to treat the way in which the USSR and its satellites were governed as a legitimate issue for American foreign policy.

Richard Nixon's policy of détente recognized the balance (or "parity") of nuclear power and gave priority to managing the competition through negotiations that produced a series of treaties limiting both strategic offensive weapons and defensive (antimissile) systems. While the arms-control process continued to be a fixture of U.S.-Soviet relations for another quarter century, détente came to be widely seen as a twentieth-century American version of nineteenth-century European realpolitik. As such, it came under domestic attack. During Nixon's scandal-ridden and truncated second term, he came under pressure from a variety of quarters to empower the Conference on Security and Cooperation in Europe (CSCE).

CSCE originated as a Kremlin initiative. It was intended to consolidate and secure recognition of the Soviet occupation of Eastern Europe. The long-running negotiation brought together members of the Warsaw Pact and NATO, along with other European states. It covered disarmament, trade and "cultural" issues, and human rights as well. The initiative rebounded against the USSR when the West turned CSCE into a platform for criticizing Communist regimes for violating the human rights of their citizens. Gerald Ford inherited a U.S. position in the CSCE that led to an agreement, signed in Helsinki in 1975, that committed all signatories to respect freedom of expression, religion, and travel. To an extent that the Kremlin leaders did not fully

---

3 Dwight Eisenhower and Khrushchev met in 1955 as part of the "Big Four," along with the leaders of the UK and France. That phrase lived on until 1960, until the Paris four-power summit that was disrupted by U-2 affair.

recognize at the time, the USSR had allowed its domestic practices and policies to become a legitimate target of diplomatic objections from other governments.[4]

Later, the Helsinki Accords, in addition to their precedent-setting implications for the Soviet Government, gave heart to dissidents and reformers in Central and Eastern Europe. Communist governments were obliged to publish the full Helsinki text. It became a beacon and benchmark for the opponents of totalitarianism. Over time, the CSCE took on an institutional character that gave the United States and other nations of the West an established right and a readily available means to exert modest but constant influence on the Soviet Union to move toward what Kennan had called the "mellowing" of the system.

Meanwhile, on a parallel track, the United States revived John Foster Dulles's concept—though not the slogan—of rollback. Zbigniew Brzezinski, who had helped David Rockefeller found the Trilateral Commission, attended the Commission's annual meeting in Bonn in 1977 in his capacity as President Jimmy Carter's assistant for national security affairs. Brzezinski used that occasion to argue for a more assertive, competitive version of détente, one that would press for change inside Soviet-dominated countries rather than accept the status quo. This approach—with an emphasis on undermining Soviet client regimes through the support of prodemocracy movements like Solidarity in Poland and militant resistance movements like the mujahideen in Afghanistan, anti-Communist guerrillas in Angola, and the contras in Nicaragua—came into its own in the 1980s and therefore acquired the label of the "Reagan Doctrine." The Carter and Reagan administrations also stepped up American support for proponents of reform in the USSR itself—Andrei Sakharov and Anatoly (now Natan) Sharansky, for example.

The better-informed members of the Soviet political elite were coming to appreciate that their economy was in deep distress and that there was an urgent need for reform. They were impatient for the end of the

4 The final act was divided into three sections called "baskets." Basket one legitimized the boundaries established at the Yalta and Potsdam Conferences for post-World War II Europe. Basket two dealt with economic cooperation. The Soviets agreed to concessions in basket three because they thought they were getting—in baskets one's recognition of the postwar borders of Poland and the division of Germany—the better end of the bargain.

long, gray "era of stagnation" under Leonid Brezhnev's gerontocracy. In the early 1980s, Brezhnev, Yuri Andropov, and Konstantin Chernenko died in rapid succession, each after a period of on-the-job decrepitude. In 1985, the Politburo picked the 54-year-old Mikhail Gorbachev to revitalize the country. The Politburo—and Gorbachev—got more than they bargained for. Gorbachev substituted perestroika (restructuring) for the iron fist of Soviet rule and glasnost (openness) for the Big Lie. To concentrate on modernizing the society and open the Soviet Union to the world, he sued for peace in the Cold War. In a conversation with a presidential emissary from Washington in June 1989, a little more than four months before the Berlin Wall came down, Gorbachev introduced a new word—significantly, one borrowed from English—to describe his vision for relations with the United States: *partnyorstvo,* or partnership.[5] To Gorbachev and his advisers, it meant moving from negative peace—the avoidance of a cataclysmic conflict—to joint efforts between the superpowers, based on the recognition that they had compatible interests as well as competing ones.

President Reagan, more than most of his own aides, was prepared to test how far the Soviets were willing to go in translating the concept of partnership into action. His successor, George H. W. Bush, picked up where Reagan left off in looking for ways to give substance to the idea of U.S.-Soviet partnership. To an extent that would have been unimaginable during the Cold War, Bush tried to take Gorbachev's domestic problems into account in the way he prosecuted—and ended—the first Gulf War in 1991, and he brought the Soviet Union into the Middle East peace process as a cosponsor of the Madrid Conference.

During those turbulent years, Bush as well as the other leaders of the G-7 major industrialized democracies saw Gorbachev as a dramatically new—indeed transformational—kind of Soviet leader. Therefore they invited him to be their guest in London for part of their annual summit in mid-July 1991. Bush assumed the role of a supportive, steady, attentive, highly competent air-traffic controller guiding Gorbachev as he piloted the Soviet Union in for a soft landing on the ash heap of history. Within six months of Gorbachev's appearance at the London G-7, he gave up his place in the Kremlin to Boris Yeltsin, the first elected

---

5 Gorbachev first used the term with Admiral William Crowe, chairman of the Joint Chiefs of Staff in the Reagan administration on June 21, 1989. Crowe was in Moscow reciprocating a visit that his Soviet counterpart, Marshal Sergei Akhromeyev, had made to the United States.

president of Russia. Once that happened, Bush wasted no time in establishing strong personal ties to the new man in the Kremlin. As a result, during the 1992 presidential election in the United States, Yeltsin was clearly rooting for Bush.

Bill and Boris

Bill Clinton, literally from his first day in office, set about forming his own close bond with Yeltsin (they spoke by phone within hours of Clinton's inauguration). For the next eight years, Clinton gave more attention to the management of relations with Russia than with any other country. Personal diplomacy with Yeltsin was, for Clinton, the principal way of keeping that relationship on an even course during a period of wrenching transition and frequent upheaval inside Russia. Supporting Yeltsin against a Communist comeback was one of Clinton's major objectives.

Building on a program inherited from the Bush administration, Clinton increased the level of technical assistance for Russian efforts to create institutions of democratic governance and civil society, particularly at the grassroots level and in the far reaches of the country. He also worked with other leading developed democracies to generate multilateral financial support through the World Bank, the IMF, and the European Bank for Reconstruction and Development (EBRD).

Clinton's other goal was to encourage the development of a truly post-Soviet Russian foreign policy. That meant inducing Russia to respect the sovereignty of its newly independent neighbors and, in particular, removing its troops from the Baltic states, supporting Western efforts to bring peace in the Balkans, accepting the right of former Soviet satellites and republics to join NATO, and entering into a "NATO-Russia permanent joint council." After considerable resistance and at great cost domestically, Yeltsin agreed on all counts.

Partly for that reason—but also because of ill health, a shattered economy, and a seemingly nonstop struggle with his opponents—Yeltsin, by 1999, was a spent force. He ceded much of his authority to his prime minister and heir designate, Vladimir Putin. Putin's rise coincided with a new outbreak of war in and around Chechnya. Trouble in that corner of the Russian Federation not only constituted a recurrent, potentially chronic crisis in its own right; it also represented a more general threat to Russia's transition from dictatorship to democracy. Chechen secessionism provoked repressive instincts on the part of the Russian leadership and discriminatory ones among ethnic Russians, not just toward the Chechens but toward other minorities as well. Also, the reliance of the Chechens on foreign help in their struggle, as well as safe havens in neighboring countries, especially Georgia, provided Moscow with a national-security pretext for asserting special rights in "the near abroad," a term that took in all of the former Soviet republics. Most significantly, the hazard that Chechen separatists posed to Moscow's authority and to Russia's sovereignty and territorial integrity played into Putin's desire to reverse the diffusion of power and the opening-up of the Russian political system and society that had, in his view—and in the view of many Russians—gone too far under Yeltsin.

At the end of the Clinton administration, there was concern in Washington that Putin's concept of a strong state could be achieved only at the expense of a burgeoning civil society, vigorous free media, and progress, however erratic, toward a robust democracy. For his part, Putin was polite, even deferential, in his own dealings with Clinton, but he was unwilling to do any real business with an American president who was in his last year in office. Putin was waiting to see who would win the U.S. election in 2000. He hinted, and some of his aides made clear, that they were hoping that the next American president would be George W. Bush, who was stressing a theme of neo-Nixonian realpolitik in his campaign and who would therefore be more pragmatic about Russian domestic politics than Al Gore. To many Russians, that meant the Republicans would recognize Putin's need to impose order on the chaos of the Yeltsin years.

The 1990s were indeed a time of great hardship for many Russians and there have been, since Putin took over from Yeltsin, improvements for which he deserves credit. There have also been points of continuity between Yeltsin and Putin, although they were more pronounced during Putin's first term. For example, both Yeltsin and Putin continued to use Gorbachev's term, "partnership," for Russia's relationship with the United States—and with the EU as well.

Yeltsin and Putin also built on Gorbachev's participation in G-7 meetings. After making sure that that invitation became an annual tradition, Yeltsin pressed for full membership in a new G-8—or, as he called it, the Vosmyorka (the Big Eight). He got his wish in 1998. Early in Putin's own presidency, he adopted a particularly striking word:

zapadnichestvo, which conveys a belief in Russia's Western vocation. For Yeltsin and Putin, the G-8 did triple duty: it served to advance their country's uniquely important bilateral relationship with the United States; it helped solidify Russia's ties to Canada, Europe, and Japan; and it gave credibility to Russia's claim to a position of global leadership since the G-8 is widely seen—and sees itself—as a de facto board of directors of the world order (a perception that is shared, albeit resentfully, by countries like China, India, and Brazil that aspire to membership in an expanded version of the G-8).

Yet among the members of the Big Eight, the relationship between the United States and Russia was still unique. The United States, according to the cliché, was the world's sole remaining superpower (the Big One), while Russia had, in its own view particularly, the dubious distinction of being a former superpower. Even shorn of its satellites and 14 other former Soviet republics, it still extended across two continents and 11 times zones, bordered on 14 countries, possessed reserves of at least 69 billion barrels of oil and 47 trillion cubic meters of natural gas, and had an arsenal of about 16,000 nuclear weapons. But all those statistical superlatives did not make Russia feel any less diminished by the loss of its superpower status nor any less fixated on the United States. The "bilats" between the U.S. and Russian leaders that always took place "on the margins" of the G-8 were, for the Russians, a means of maintaining the impression that the common denominator of international numerology was still the Big Two.

The three American presidents who have dealt with Russia since 1991—the first President Bush, Bill Clinton, and George W. Bush—have, to put it mildly, had their differences. That goes for "Bush41," the arch-multilateralist, and "Bush43," who, during his first term, was unabashedly unilateralist. But in their policies toward Russia, all three have sought to translate the rhetoric of partnership and the fact of Russia's membership in the G-8 into broad-based collaboration based not just on shared interests but also on shared values.

Of those values, the most important are the ones associated with the last word in the full name of the G-8: its members are supposed to be the world's major industrialized democracies. In the eyes of the leaders of the old G-7, the president of Russia earned a place in their company in part because he was elected to an office that had previously been held by an appointee of the Politburo. At the same time, they recognized that a country that had never known anything but dictatorship, even if its citizens suddenly had the right to vote, could not, overnight, become a mature democracy. They reached out first to Gorbachev and then to Yeltsin because, under their leadership, Russia had changed course and was now, finally, moving in the right direction: namely, toward becoming, over time, a country where citizens have a variety of choices, both in candidates and in parties; where citizens form their own opinions by sifting through a wide array of information, analysis, and commentary coming from free media; where they have no reason to fear the consequence of peaceful opposition to government policy; where pluralism is institutionalized in governing structures and respected in the nongovernmental sector; where there is a system of checks and balances to guard against the concentration or abuse of political power; and, crucially, where there is rule of law, including protection against and punishment of systemic corruption.

The rationale for giving Russia the status of a regular guest at the G-7 and later of full membership in the G-8 was reinforced by its government's accession to other accords such as Statute of the Council of Europe and the Convention for the Protection of Human Rights and Fundamental Freedoms, both of which Russia ratified in 1996. In the two years that followed, Russia also ratified 11 protocols elaborating on the obligations that the convention entails.

At the G-7+1 summits between 1991 and 1997 and the five G-8s since 1998, Gorbachev, Yeltsin, and Putin signed a series of documents committing themselves to strengthening good governance, rule of law, civil society, and respect for human rights and national minorities.[6] Explicit guarantees of the freedom of the press and the "democratic accountability" (that is, the independence) of the judiciary were added at Putin's own first G-8—and Bill Clinton's last—in Okinawa in 2000.

By then, however, Clinton had already begun to voice his suspicion that Putin was "good at talking the right talk while walking in the wrong direction." In June 2000, immediately after his first meeting in the Kremlin with Putin as the newly elected president of Russia, Clinton visited Yeltsin, then living in retirement outside Moscow. Clinton told Yeltsin that he had doubts about whether Putin was "a real democrat and a real reformer."

---

6 See, for example, the statements released at the Denver G-7 summit, with Yeltsin in attendance, in 1997; and at the G-8 summits in Birmingham in 1998 and Köln in 1999 (again, with Yeltsin present); followed by those in Okinawa in 2000 and Genoa in 2001, with Putin representing Russia.

George and Vladimir

George W. Bush came into office with a view of the world and of U.S. interests with regard to Russia quite different from Clinton's—and, indeed, from all his predecessors. For one thing, Bush was skeptical if not disdainful of the arms-control negotiations that had figured so prominently on the agenda of U.S.-Soviet/Russian relations since the 1960s. He was eager to develop and deploy a national missile defense system of a type and on a scale prohibited by the Anti-Ballistic Missile (ABM) Treaty that Nixon and Brezhnev had signed nearly three decades before. Insofar as Bush thought at all about Russia in his first months in office, the matter most on his mind was how to minimize Putin's objections to the scrapping of the ABM Treaty.

Bush did not regard Russia's troubled internal transition as a major concern for the United States. Instead, he saw it as an open-ended preoccupation for the Kremlin that would prevent leaders there from constituting a major threat to U.S. geopolitical interests any time soon. Russia went from being a top strategic priority of the U.S. government to being, at best, a middle-rank issue. Many Russians regarded this new, relaxed, detached American attitude as exasperating if not insulting, since it confirmed their loss of superpower status. Putin, however, reacted with his characteristic calm. He may even have welcomed an opportunity to distinguish himself from Yeltsin and to demonstrate that he was not overly dependent on the United States. Indeed, neither he nor Bush wanted to replicate the Bill-and-Boris special relationship that had so dominated much of the previous decade—or, for that matter, the George-and-Boris and George-and-Mikhail ones that had preceded it.

As it happened, the U.S.-Russian experiment with presidential standoffishness was short-lived. When Putin had a chance to meet with Bush, in Ljubljana in June 2001, he drew on his considerable skills to ingratiate himself with the new U.S. leader. Bush said publicly that he had "looked the man in the eye. I found him to be very straightforward and trustworthy . . . I was able to get a sense of his soul; a man deeply committed to his country and the best interests of his country." A major reason for Bush's satisfaction with the meeting was Putin's seemingly relaxed attitude toward the new administration's enthusiasm for national missile defense. Another point on which they agreed, at least implicitly, was the desirability of reducing the extent to which Russia's internal developments figured in—and complicated—government-to-government dealings.

The terror attacks of September 11, 2001, strengthened the Bush-Putin relationship. Less than an hour after the first airliner slammed into the World Trade Center, Putin was the first foreign leader to phone Bush. He offered more cooperation and support than Bush even asked for. Putin weathered some domestic criticism for giving a green light to the stationing of U.S. troops in Central Asia in support of operations in Afghanistan. Putin, according to several associates with whom we have spoken, thought he had at least a tacit understanding with Bush: the Kremlin would show forbearance with regard to the expansion of American military power into what had traditionally been Russia's sphere of influence; in exchange the White House would refrain from criticizing Putin for his efforts to reestablish a strong centralized state in general and, in particular, Russia's scorched-earth policies in conflict with the ongoing resistance in Chechnya.

For Bush, the Cold War was not only over—it had been replaced in American strategic thinking by the war on terror, and Bush saw Putin as an ally. That made Bush all the more inclined to reduce the extent to which Putin's internal policies figured in—and complicated—their dealings. It was in the wake of 9/11 that Bush and Putin moved comfortably onto a first-name basis.

That personal rapport contributed to Bush's willingness to award Putin a prize long coveted by the Kremlin—the chairmanship of the G-8. Washington reversed its previous position (shared by a majority of the G-7) that Russia should not take the chair until the country's political and economic development equipped it for the role and until Russia had become a member of the WTO and OECD. In July 2002—only 10 months after 9/11—when the Big Eight met in Kananaskis, Alberta, they announced that the 2006 gathering would be in Russia. Putin proposed as a venue St. Petersburg, his hometown and the incubator of his transformation from a relatively junior KGB officer to the strong right arm of a reformist mayor, Anatoly Sobchak (his loyalty and efficiency in that post had brought him to Yeltsin's attention).

By agreeing to meet in St. Petersburg, the G-8 would be reaffirming its confidence about the path along which Russia was moving and its approval of Putin as the country's leader. The statement issued in Kananaskis said as much: "Russia has demonstrated its potential to play a full and meaningful role in addressing the global problems that we all face. This decision reflects the remarkable economic and *democratic transformation* that has occurred in Russia in recent years *and in particular under the leadership of President Putin."*

Within two years, American officials at a high level were privately expressing regret over the language italicized in the preceding passage—and, indeed, second thoughts about the decision itself. It was increasingly apparent that in two of Putin's signature phrases, "managed democracy" and "dictatorship of law," the accent was on the first word. The jailing of Mikhail Khodorkovsky in October 2003 and the systematic dismantlement of Khodorkovsky's Yukos was especially jarring for those in the higher reaches of the U.S. government who had, until then, given Putin the benefit of rising doubts about whether he was truly a modernizer. To those, like Bush's then national security adviser, Condoleezza Rice, who knew Russia (and Russian) well, the Khodorkovsky affair smacked of an especially ugly word for an atavistic—and Soviet—practice: *proizvol,* the arbitrary, despotic use of political power to punish those whom the Kremlin sees as enemies.

Even then, however, Bush himself was reluctant to speak out publicly on the worrisome drift of events in Russia or even press his concerns vigorously in private with Putin. That was largely because, in 2003 and 2004, the American president and his administration had their hands full with the occupation of Iraq. With Russia giving the United States less of a hard time on that subject than some American allies, Bush chose to play down growing concerns about Putin's domestic policies. When Bush hosted the G-8 in Sea Island, Georgia, in July 2004, he settled for a summit statement that was noticeably silent on the political and civic values that supposedly united the group.

After the Beslan debacle in early September of 2004, Bush used his annual speech to the General Assembly of the United Nations to express outrage at the perpetrators and sympathy for the victims. He said nothing, however, about the way Putin was using the tragedy to step up a five-year campaign to reestablish Russia as a highly centralized, vertical state with power concentrated in the Kremlin, and how this development fit into Putin's ongoing effort to regulate and manipulate the dissemination of information. During this period, officials in Moscow let it be known that they regarded the Bush administration as more "understanding" than the EU, where concern about developments in Russia was on the rise. Putin himself all but endorsed Bush for reelection.[7]

The contrast in U.S. foreign policy between the first and second George W. Bush terms is rare, perhaps even unprecedented, in the annals of the American presidency. There has been a shift toward a greater a reliance on diplomacy, consultation with allies, and respect for international institutions. With regard to Russia, the administration has elevated the attention it has given to internal developments, including those that do not support the president's desire to see—and treat—Putin as a partner. One reason is that Bush listened to his closest ally. Shortly after Bush's reelection, Prime Minister Tony Blair privately warned of looming difficulties with "our friend Vladimir." Even before Bush's second inauguration, there were signals from the White House—and, crucially, from the State Department as it prepared to welcome Rice as the new secretary—that the administration realized, with more clarity than before, that it had what one senior official called a "Putin problem," and that the results of the "embrace" of Putin during the first term had turned out to be "disappointing."

On the eve of a bilateral summit in Bratislava, Slovakia, in February 2005, Bush and Putin sparred publicly. "For Russia to make progress as a European nation, the Russian government must renew its commitment to democracy and the rule of law," said Bush. "The United States and all European countries should place democratic reform at the heart of their dialogue with Russia." Putin shot back that "the fundamental principles of democracy and the institutions of democracy must be adapted to the reality of today's life in Russia, to our traditions and history." The debate was played out in private as well, although they tried, none too convincingly, to keep up appearances of what they called a "strong U.S.-Russian partnership" on security cooperation and counterterrorism.

---

7 During the Sea Island summit of the G-8—shortly before the Republican Party convention—Putin accused Democrats of hypocrisy for their criticism of Bush's invasion of Iraq. He noted that it had been a Democrat (Clinton) who had bombed Yugoslavia in 1999, implying that Bush's war against Iraq was no different. On October 18, 2004, two weeks before Election Day, Putin said if Bush were voted out of office, it "could lead to the spread of terrorism to other parts of the world . . . International terrorists have set as their goal inflicting the maximum damage to Bush, to prevent his election to a second term. If they succeed in doing that, they will celebrate a victory over America and over the entire anti-terror coalition."

Bush came home from Bratislava sharing a view that we heard in a number of Trilateral capitals as we prepared this report: a number of aides and advisers to Western and Japanese leaders privately said that they wished this year's G-8 were taking place somewhere other than on Russian territory and with someone other than Putin in the role of chairman.

As President Bush approached St. Petersburg, he faced a dilemma. His father was instrumental in inviting Gorbachev to attend the G-7 as a guest; his predecessor, Bill Clinton, was instrumental in bringing Russia into the G-8; and Bush himself gave the go-ahead to Putin's chairing the St. Petersburg meeting and thereby allowing him to set—and thus limit—the agenda to a trio of global issues: energy security, infectious diseases, and education. While important, those topics were clearly chosen to make it as difficult as possible for anyone to criticize what is going on inside Russia. If Bush and the other six visitors played their roles in St. Petersburg entirely by the Russian script, they would be letting Putin turn the event into a collective endorsement of trends that are incompatible with, if not anathema to, the principles of governance and international behavior that the G-8 supposedly stands for.

On the other hand, cancellation of the St. Petersburg summit—a course of action advocated by a bipartisan group of American legislators—was out of the question from the standpoint of the G-7. Moreover, as some outspoken critics of Russia's "de-democratization" acknowledged, it made no sense.[8] "Putinism" is popular in Russia. Indeed, some version of "Putinism," with another name attached, will

---

8 Starting in 2003, bills were introduced in both the U.S. House of Representatives and the U.S. Senate to urge the suspension of Russia from the G-8 "until the Russian Government ends its assault on democracy and political freedom." The Senate version (S.Con.Res.85) was put forward by John McCain and Joseph Lieberman, who would soon be joined by more senators of both parties who wanted to add their names as cosponsors: Evan Bayh (D-IN), Conrad Burns (R-MT), Saxby Chambliss (R-GA), Gordon Smith (R-OR), and Richard Durban (D-IL). In the House, an identical bill (H.Con.Res.336) was coauthored by Democrat Tom Lantos, the ranking minority member of the International Relations Committee, and Republican Christopher Cox, the chairman of the Committee on Homeland Security. In February 2006, at the annual Wehrkunde Conference on Security Policy in Munich, McCain followed up by remarking that "seriously question[ed] whether the G-8 leaders should attend the St. Petersburg summit." *(continued on next page)*

likely be popular after Putin leaves the scene. That makes the G-8's so-called Putin problem really a Russia problem—and therefore a more complex challenge for the West, not to mention for Russian democrats and reformers. A meeting that turned acrimonious over how Putin is governing his own country and pursuing what he sees as Russia's interests along its periphery would embarrass and anger not only Putin; it would have the same effect on the large majority of Russians who support the policies for which his guests in July would be taking him to task.

During the remainder of Putin's presidency and under any imaginable successor, a Russia that sees itself as marginalized or punished will be all the less inclined to orient itself toward the West. Russia's eviction from the G-8, before or after St. Petersburg, would play into the hands of nationalist forces in Russia who believe in their country's uniquely Eurasian destiny, which implies an authoritarian domestic order and a foreign policy that combines intimidation of other former Soviet republics and xenophobia toward the outside world. A signal that the West is giving up on Russia would also discourage democrats, who are down but not out.

Even if Putin used the St. Petersburg summit to make reassuring, G-8-friendly statements about his policies and intentions, that would not be grounds for relief or optimism. Another display of his knack for smooth, soothing talk would, rightly, occasion considerable skepticism, especially absent agreement on what the words he uses really mean. While radiating hospitality and statesmanship, Putin was sure to be on his guard against even gentle remonstrations from Bush. Here, too, he would have the support of many of his people.

So Bush knew that his leverage over Putin was limited. No matter how the U.S. president played the St. Petersburg meeting—hard or soft—or how he tried to split the difference, he would be criticized by Americans and Russians alike.

(Note 8 continued) The phrase "de-democratization" featured prominently in a bipartisan task force report, *Russia's Wrong Direction: What the United States Can and Should Do,* issued by the New York-based Council on Foreign Relations in March 2006, www.cfr.org/content/publications/attachments/Russia_TaskForce.pdf. The project was chaired by former senator John Edwards and former member of the House of Representatives Jack Kemp, and was directed by Stephen Sestanovich of Council on Foreign Relations.

And then, to complicate matters further, there was the Iran factor. U.S.-Russian summits (and earlier U.S.-Soviet ones) have often been a reminder of the adage that, in diplomacy as in other areas of life, the urgent tends to drive out the merely important. St. Petersburg was no exception. For Bush, while he now recognized the ominous importance of Russian domestic trends, the Iranian nuclear program was truly urgent. So, therefore, was the task of eliciting as much cooperation as possible from Putin in galvanizing a single, forceful position within the United Nations Security Council. That argued for keeping the meeting as free from frictions and distractions as possible.

In early May, the U.S. administration took what it saw as a step toward easing its predicament by having Vice President Dick Cheney deliver a speech that laid out, in blunt terms, the case for concern about Russia's direction:

> [I]n Russia today, opponents of reform are seeking to reverse the gains of the last decade. In many areas of civil society—from religion and the news media, to advocacy groups and political parties—the government has unfairly and improperly restricted the right of her people. Other actions by the Russian government have been counterproductive, and could begin to affect relations with other countries. No legitimate interest is served when oil and gas become tools of intimidation or blackmail, either by supply manipulation or attempts to monopolize transportation. And no one can justify actions that undermine the territorial integrity of a neighbor, or interfere with democratic movements.

Then, looking ahead, Cheney struck a guardedly positive note:

> None of us believes that Russia is fated to become an enemy. A Russia that increasingly shares the values of [the] community [of democracies] can be a strategic partner and a trusted friend as we work toward common goals.

But even these words, while conciliatory, served to distance the administration from a long-established premise of U.S.-Russian relations. Cheney was now speaking of Russia as a partner not in the present tense but in the future conditional: only a Russia that shared certain values could be a true partner, while he had just said that the Russia that Bush would soon be visiting was decreasingly meeting the standard for partnership.

Kremlin officials protested—some vociferously, some with sarcasm, while the Russian media erupted with charges that Cheney with declaring a new cold war. Every bit as provocative as the content of the speech was its venue: Vilnius, the capital of Lithuania, a former Soviet republic that was now a member of NATO and the EU. While hints at official American "disappointment" in Putin had already exacerbated the reciprocal problem of growing Russian disillusionment with the United States and suspicion about its motives, Cheney's gloves-off censure and the Russian reaction to it escalated tension between Washington and Moscow to a new level.

Several administration officials explained that the vice president's speech was an attempt to vent high-level American disapproval of trends in Russia ahead of the G-8 and thereby "inoculate" President Bush from U.S. domestic criticism for going to the summit. Perhaps, they hoped, now that the vice president had played the bad cop in Vilnius, it might be easier for the president to play the good cop, face to face with Putin, in St. Petersburg, especially on the subject of Iran.

The flap over the speech died down relatively quickly. When Putin delivered his annual address to the Russian Federal Assembly shortly after Cheney's speech, he took a swipe at the United States for being hypocritical about crusading for democracy and human rights in some countries while coddling dictators when it suited American interests to do so—and for being like "the wolf who knows whom to eat . . . and is not about to listen to anyone" (a characteristic, one might add, that wolves share with bears). But this passage in Putin's address was brief and buried deep in a speech devoted overwhelmingly to other, primarily domestic issues (the economy and the demographic crisis). Putin was in his cool-customer mode, letting the Russian media rail against Cheney while he gave the Vilnius speech the back of his hand.

Cheney's grammatical fine-tuning of "partnership" was of little interest to Putin. After all, that word—a bit like "democracy" and "reform"—had already turned sour in Russian mouths; it was, as we heard during our own visits to Moscow, increasingly uttered with sarcasm, even bitterness. Many Russians, including quite a few who consider themselves liberals, believe that partnership has meant serial capitulation: to the first President Bush on the unification of Germany within NATO; to President Clinton on the enlargement of NATO and the U.S.-led war that the alliance waged against Serbia; to the second President Bush on the U.S. withdrawal from the ABM Treaty and the stationing of U.S. troops in the Caucasus and Central Asia.

As for American criticism of what is happening to their politics, many Russians—again, including some, perhaps many, who have misgivings of their own about Putin's course—feel that it is exaggerated, simplistic, and based on the arrogant assumption that the United States has the perfect model of democracy and the right to impose it on others. In Moscow, we heard quite a bit of schadenfreude about the Bush administration's inadvertent promotion of illiberal democracy—and, more to the point, Islamic fundamentalists acquiring political power through the ballot box—in Egypt, the Palestinian Authority, and Iraq. We also heard accusations that American invocations of democratic values and foreign-policy norms constitute a smoke screen for a strategy aimed, not at fostering Russian democracy at all, but at keeping Russia weak. Quite a few of our interlocutors asserted—some in sorrow, some in anger—that the U.S.-Russian relationship has moved into a new, fundamentally competitive phase.

What Is to Be Done?

When Cheney subtly but unmistakably downgraded "partnership" in the vocabulary of U.S.-Russian relations in his Vilnius speech, he implied a substitute concept by giving prominence to a word that we have used several times in this report and that is echoed in its title. "[T]he leading industrialized nations will engage Russia at the Group of Eight Summit," said the vice president. "Engagement" is, indeed, a term better suited to the possibilities and limitations of the relationship. It reflects the need for increased exchange programs that will give Russians a chance to work, study, and travel abroad and enable foreign executives to work with Russian firms and foreign teachers and students to spend time in Russian universities. In the realm of diplomacy and security cooperation, engagement, like partnership, connotes a steady, proactive search for areas where American and Russian interests and perceptions coincide. But unlike partnership—which suggests that the partners should bend over backward to appear to be agreeing and cooperating even when they are at odds—engagement suggests a high degree of candor and realism when interests and perceptions diverge. Realism in this context means recognizing that officials in Moscow, like those of any country, make decisions and set policy on the basis of national interest. The principal issues on which Russia—and

Putin—should be engaged can be cast in those terms, including the three topics that Putin has put on the agenda for St. Petersburg:

- For Russia to achieve energy security for itself and to contribute to energy security for the rest of the world, it will have to forswear the use of enterprises like Gazprom as instruments of state power to put political pressure on neighbors like Ukraine; and it will have to promote transparency and world-standard corporate governance in the Russian energy sector.
- For Russia to deal effectively with infectious diseases within its own borders, it will need to display much more transparency in its dealings with international health agencies.
- For Russia to benefit from the global push for more effective support of education, it will have to open its own universities to financial and technical assistance from, and exchanges with, the outside world. That will mean protecting Russian higher education from xenophobic restrictions on NGOs.

The harder task will be addressing the difficult subjects that Putin does not want to talk about in St. Petersburg or anywhere else: the defederalization of a state that still calls itself a federation; the reconcentration of power at the center and at the top; the near-total crackdown on the electronic media; the creeping squeeze on political opposition and elimination of checks and balances; support for reactionary, oppressive regimes in some neighboring states; and the subversion of democratic elections in others. On all these issues, one point can be forcefully argued: those trends—which make Russia today less qualified for membership in, not to mention chairmanship of, the G-8 than it was when Putin became president—will, if they continue, weaken the Russian state, thereby making a mockery of what Putin clearly wants to be his legacy. The overreliance on high oil prices and the delusion that Russia can become a petro superpower have become an excuse for failing to diversify and modernize the economy, thus missing an opportunity to attract far more foreign investment. Massive, escalating official and judicial corruption further weakens Russia's ability to compete in the global marketplace.

It might be helpful for those Russians who benefit from corrupt practices to be reminded that the rule of law is alive and well in the countries where they like to vacation and stash their money. The day may be coming when they will not be able to berth their yachts in Mediterranean marinas or ski in the Alps without the risk of being arrested by local authorities. While Russia's ruling and privileged classes—which are increasingly overlapping categories—may be correct that it is time to move "beyond partnership" with the West, they have neither the desire nor the ability to withdraw from a globalized world. And that means living by uniform rules and norms—which is, or should be, what the G-8 is all about.

The need for all eight members to come to grips with that fact will persist as long as they remain a "group" with a capital G, whose leaders meet annually with great fanfare and under considerable scrutiny. To the extent that the St. Petersburg meeting soft-pedals the awkward but inescapable fact that Russia is less open, pluralistic, and democratic—and more corrupt and authoritarian—than it was a few years ago, there will be all the more pressure, within the G-7 countries, to deal more straightforwardly with that set of issues a year from now, at the next G-8.

Fortuitously, the 2007 meeting will be held in the German seaside resort of Heiligendamm, with Chancellor Angela Merkel in the chair. She can speak to Putin in Russian just as he was able to speak to her predecessor, Gerhard Schröder, in German. On visits to Moscow, she has made a point of meeting with reformers and democrats, in part to demonstrate that they are not being forgotten in the West—and their fate, if they come to harm, will not be ignored.

There is an interesting and potentially useful symmetry between Merkel and Putin. Each of them knows both of the other's countries—that is, the defunct ones where they grew up (the GDR and USSR), and the ones they now lead (the unified FRG and the Russian Federation). With Merkel's intimate knowledge of Russia's past and her intuitive appreciation of the extent to which Russia's future is bound up with the future of Europe, the Heiligendamm G-8 could be a dramatic and, from Putin's perspective, unwelcome contrast to his G-8 in St. Petersburg. She will have as much influence over the agenda next year as he had this year.

That prospect might create an opportunity to use the Heiligendamm G-8 to review the implementation of various principles that all eight governments have agreed to at previous meetings and other settings over the past 15 years. Over the coming year, quiet diplomacy might help the Big Eight agree on definitions of what those joint obligations should mean in practice, as well as timetables, benchmarks, and mechanisms for monitoring progress. If the task the G-8 sets itself for 2007 and beyond is put in terms of delivering on existing commitments by all members, the Russians cannot legitimately complain that their country is being subjected to new demands or discriminatory conditions.

In the spring of 2006, we found among quite a few of our German colleagues skepticism about whether Chancellor Merkel will have the necessary combination of political will, domestic backing, and support from her West European colleagues to take the lead in administering tough love to Putin a year from now. According to one strain of conventional wisdom, she—and they—will feel they must give priority to dealing with Russia as a source of oil and gas. Once again, it is predicted, the urgent will drive out the important; once again, geopolitics—or geoeconomics—will trump the West's stake in Russia's internal development.

We hope not, for if the G-8 again evades or downplays a core issue about itself—that is, whether the members are all democracies—its very future will be in doubt, and deservedly so. The G-8 may wither away and the G-7 may reemerge as the elite grouping where real business gets done, perhaps to be supplanted by a larger G that reflects the growing importance of emerging powers in Asia, Africa, and Latin America. The seven would be bear responsibility for that outcome. The United States will bear particular responsibility: no matter where the G-8 meets, the United States is still the Big One. Merkel is far more likely to follow her instincts and prove the skeptics wrong if she has the support of Bush, who will be nearing the last year of his presidency and looking to shore up his legacy and vindicate his championship of democracy.

But if the Heiligendamm G-8 were to be the last such meeting, the biggest loser would be Russia. In addition to the negative trends over which Putin has already presided, there would be another particularly ironic one: Russia's self-demotion as a major power with a seat at the table of the world's self-styled board of directors. With him in the Kremlin, Russia would have reached a summit on his own terms and his own turf, but it would be downhill from there. And that would be in nobody's interest.

6

Russia and Europe: Old Neighbors and New

> What is Russia today for Europe? It is at the same time a neighbor, a partner, a competitor, a source of concern, a threat (the approach of some new Member States), a source of uncertainty, a counterweight to American power in the multipolar perspective.
>
> What does Russia want from its relations with the EU? Russia is torn between, on the one hand, a strong geopolitical attraction to Western Europe, a real interest in its know-how and technical creativity and, on the other, distrust of Europe's political culture.
>
> —Report to the French National Assembly[1]
> December 2004

Europe's perspective on Russia diverges from the perspectives of North America and Asia for obvious reasons. Russia is not merely a neighbor: it is part of the European continent and family of peoples in a way that it will never be part of Asia, even though two-thirds of the Russian landmass technically lies within Asia. Ethnic Russians (who make up an estimated 80 percent or more of the population of the Russian Federation) trace their origins to Slavic tribes that migrated from Central and Eastern Europe in the first millennium. With over 100 million Russian citizens living in European Russia, Russia is by a margin the larg-

1 Translated from "Les relations entre l'Union européene et la Russie: quel avenir?" Foreign Affairs Committee of the National Assembly; presented by Deputies René André and Jean-Louis Bianco.

> If the US-Russia relationship may be likened to that of two planets affecting various degrees of push and pull forces on each other, then EU-Russia relations resemble a shattered universe of confusing and complex forces of influence . . . The current US agenda is "thin", focusing on a limited number of areas of relevance to US interests . . . By contrast, the EU agenda with Russia remains "thick", starting with deep energy ties and economic relations to various forms of political interaction . . . Whereas Russia only matters episodically for the United States, Russia matters almost across the board for the EU.
>
> —Dov Lynch
> "Same View, Different Realities" in
> *Friends Again? EU-US Relations after the Crisis*
> Institute for Security Studies, European Union

est European nation. The Russian Orthodox Church—one of the defining elements of Russian culture and national identity—accurately reflects Russia's bipolar relationship with Europe: the Church is part of European Christendom and has a close affinity (plus a degree of sibling rivalry) with other Orthodox churches, but it stands apart from Catholicism and Protestantism and is hostile to their entry onto its sovereign territory.

As the quotation at the opening of the chapter indicates, various factors shape the European view of Russia, and there are some fairly sharp differences of view within Western and Central Europe. The intertwining of Russian and Western European culture over the past three centuries, which not even the dark age of Communism could disrupt, has had a universally positive effect. Trade has also been a positive factor, especially for countries such as Germany, Finland, and Italy, which have been particularly successful in the Russian market. The EU is by far Russia's largest trading partner (although the reverse is not the case), and London has become the center for Russia's international financial business. This inevitably gives Europe a different perspective from that of the United States, whose trade with Russia is smaller (over 50 percent of Russian exports go to the EU, around 7 percent to the United States).

The influence of geopolitics is less positive, with Europe having been the front line of the Cold War and with nine EU members or candidate members and the Eastern *Länder* of Germany having bitter memories of a half century under Soviet occupation. Europe would feel most directly the effects of any instability in Russia (in 1992, for example, Central Europe was bracing itself for a wave of economic migrants from Russia) and is already feeling the effects of instability in the "post-Soviet space." What happens in Belarus or Ukraine is of vital interest, for example, to Poland, which borders both countries and has a substantial national minority in Belarus.

In this chapter we shall explore, first, how European attitudes toward Russia have evolved since the end of the Cold War; second, the nature of institutional relationships embracing the EU, NATO, the OSCE and the Council of Europe; and finally, issues for the future.

Europe's Perspective on Russia since the Cold War

Events spreading from within Russia in the mid-1980s, originally from within the Kremlin walls, triggered the most dramatic and unexpected changes on the continent of Europe since the end of the Second World War. Mikhail Gorbachev was hailed as a hero in Western Europe (to the majority of his fellow countrymen he is the reverse.). The fall of the Berlin Wall, the liberation of Central and Eastern Europe, and the opening up of Russia to normal contact of every kind created the most exciting possibilities. At a stroke, the Cold War became the peace dividend.

The euphoric dawn of a new age was followed rapidly by a rude awakening to the massive difficulty of converting 400 million people from Communism to capitalism and democracy and of controlling tensions suppressed by totalitarian repression. The most spectacular consequences were the dissolution into conflict of the former Yugoslavia and the collapse of the Russian economy, with a fear that the Russian Federation would itself implode. Europe struggled to resolve the problems of the Balkans and also responded energetically to requests for help in Russia. Immediate humanitarian aid (possibly misconceived but well intended) in 1992 was followed by extensive national and EU technical assistance programs,[2] the foundation of the EBRD, and European support for IMF and World Bank programs.

On the political and security fronts, Europe recognized the Russian Federation as the successor state to the rights and obligations of the Soviet Union and also responded favorably to the formation of the Commonwealth of Independent States, seeing the CIS as a factor for stabilizing relationships amid the fragmentation of the USSR. European leaders, foreign ministers, and finance ministers developed strong and supportive relationships with President Yeltsin and his team. Defense ministries changed their military doctrine and NATO redefined its role, developing the concept of Partnership for Peace. The Organization for Security and Cooperation in Europe (OSCE) gained a raft of new members and a new lease on life and engaged actively in attempts to resolve the regional conflicts that had broken out in and around the former Soviet Union and in election monitoring. For a while, in the first half of the 1990s, zero-sum diplomacy seemed to be a thing of the past. In most of these initiatives, Western Europe worked alongside the United States (their disagreements over Bosnia belong to a different narrative) and often took the lead, especially in economic matters. President Yeltsin's relationships with the leading figures of Western Europe, notably with Chancellor Kohl, were at least as close as with the U.S. president. Yeltsin was invited to summit meetings with EU heads of government and was first invited to a G-7 summit under European chairmanship at Naples in 1994. It was a shared endeavor, backed by a strong consensus within the EU.

Relations became more strained in the latter part of the decade. Mutual endeavor turned into mutual disappointment. On the Russian side, NATO's operations in the Balkans— epitomized by the bombing

---

2 From 1991 to 2006, over €7,000 million have been allocated by the EU for the Technical Assistance for the Commonwealth of Independent States (TACIS) program devoted to assist the newly created states after the breakup of the Soviet Union. The objective of this program was and still is to promote the transition to a market economy and to reinforce democracy and the rule of law in the recipient countries. The Russian Federation is the largest beneficiary of the TACIS program, having received about 40 percent of all funding, about €200 million annually. An EU Court of Auditors report published in May 2006 was highly critical of the performance of projects financed under TACIS.

of Belgrade during the Kosovo campaign and the dash of Russian SFOR troops to Pristina airport—and enlargement to include former Warsaw Pact members were deeply unpopular. Western Europe reacted against the Yeltsin government's military operation in Chechnya, beginning in 1994. The replacement of Andrei Kozyrev as Russian foreign minister in 1996 by Yevgeniy Primakov was a clear signal of a change of approach. The Europeans and Americans nevertheless worked closely with Primakov to try to head off crises over Iraq and Kosovo. They also supported Yeltsin from the sidelines in his battles with the Communists, including during the 1996 presidential election. But doubts grew about the stalling of reform in Russia, the mounting evidence of corruption and criminality, and the decay of the president and his administration. After the 1998 crash, Europe was fatigued with Russia, waiting for Yeltsin to leave the stage and hoping, with no great confidence, that Russia might then get its act together.

Putin did not at first appear to be the answer to these hopes. Commentators in the European media were mostly hostile, homing in on his KGB past, his promotion out of nowhere by Yeltsin (to whom he had granted immunity from prosecution), and the reinvasion of Chechnya under his direction. But European governments took a different view. The appearance of a new leader of a younger generation, professing the intention to integrate Russia more closely with the Western world, gave them the opportunity to reengage. Putin's first two external actions reinforced this impression. In February 2000, overriding the opposition of his own defense and foreign ministries, he closed the breach with NATO that the bombing of Serbia had created by inviting its secretary general, Lord Robertson, to Moscow and agreeing with him that the long-mooted NATO Information and Military Liaison Offices should open in the Russian capital. Putin followed this up with an invitation to the UK's prime minister, Tony Blair, to pay an informal visit to St. Petersburg; the invitation to Blair and his wife was built around the premiere of a new production of Prokofiev's opera, *War and Peace.* Putin was only the acting president. His invitation adroitly sidestepped protocol although Blair was criticized by Russian liberals and sections of the European press for agreeing to a meeting before Putin's formal election to the presidency.

The Blairs and the Putins established a warm rapport. Blair agreed to send a group of his advisers to talk to German Gref and the team preparing the reform program. He reported back favorably to his European colleagues. By the time of the Okinawa G-7/G-8 summit in the summer of 2000, all of the principal European leaders had got to know the new president. They found him a sharp contrast to his predecessor: a good listener and conversationalist, showing a sense of humor and knowledge of the world, lacking bombast, and sober. Not only his words but his policies and actions were generally encouraging although the arrest of Gusinsky (while Putin was on a visit to Spain and Germany) sounded an alarm bell. The exception to this rosy picture was that it was clear from the outset that Putin had a blind spot over Chechnya. He showed no willingness to discuss the subject frankly; instead he lapsed into a long, hard-nosed, and repetitious justification that became less and less credible as time went on. When pressed on the subject by the Western media, he several times reacted with angry emotion and barrack-room language.

Although Chechnya was to remain a neuralgic point and concerns grew about the Kremlin's growing control over television, Europe's relations with Russia progressed substantially between 2000 and 2003. Putin maintained a close relationship with Blair, which reached its apogee in the summer of 2003 when Putin became the first Russian leader for well over a century to be received in Britain on a full-dress state visit. Putin developed an even closer personal friendship with Chancellor Schröder, exploiting their ability to converse in German without need for aides or interpreters, and he developed a personal bond also with Prime Minister Berlusconi, who as president of the European Council in the autumn of 2003 was openly to contradict the EU's agreed position and give an unqualified blessing to Putin's Chechnya policy and arrest of Khodorkovsky. Relations with France were slower to bud, in part because French public opinion was sharply critical of Russian behavior in Chechnya, but they duly blossomed under the warm glow of multipolarity.

In this period, Western Europe negotiated a substantial agenda with Russia. Cooperation against terrorism deepened after September 2001, when NATO members and Russia supported or participated in the U.S.-led operation against the Taliban in Afghanistan. Russian sensitivity over the further enlargement of NATO to include the Baltic states was mitigated by an initiative started by the British prime minister and consummated at a summit in Rome (after opposition from the Pentagon had been overcome) to upgrade Russia's relations with NATO. The enlargement of the EU, which included three former Soviet republics

> Today Russia ranks as the fourth largest EU trading partner, while the EU is in first place on Russia's corresponding list. Economic ties between the EU and Russia have strengthened more rapidly over [the last 15 years] than with other regions of the world and by 2004 were worth more than 126 billion euro. The trade relationship is complementary, with Russia being the EU's most important supplier of energy, iron and steel, while the EU is among Russia's most important suppliers of telecommunications equipment, machinery and chemicals . . . By the end of 2005, ERT companies alone accounted for investments of more than 32 billion euro in Russia.
>
> *Seizing the Opportunity*
> European Round Table of Industrialists, 2006

and four former members of the Council for Mutual Economic Assistance (CMEA) and Warsaw Pact, initially looked less contentious but threw up a number of difficult issues, including access arrangements for Russia to the Kaliningrad exclave, which required transit across the new EU member state of Lithuania. Long negotiations over Russia's accession to the WTO led to an agreement in the spring of 2004, which was followed in the autumn by Russian ratification of the Kyoto Protocol. Russia expressed unhappiness about the EU's approach to Kosovo and Bosnia and withdrew its remaining forces from the Balkans, but it did not press its objections to the point of obstruction. On other issues, including nonproliferation, North Korea, the Iranian nuclear program, and the Arab-Israel dispute, European and Russian positions broadly aligned. Meanwhile, with the recovery of the Russian economy, the volume of trade and investment between the EU and Russia grew rapidly and formed the strongest bond between the Eastern and Western sides of the shared continent.

Since 2003–04, the pattern has changed. Trade and investment, apparently unaffected by politics, have continued to grow. Business-to-business relations remain extremely positive to this day. Political relations, however, have deteriorated, primarily because Europeans have drawn conclusions from events in and around Russia, including the Yukos affair, the persecution of Khodorkovsky, curbs on liberal politicians and media, brutal tactics in Chechnya, and coercion of Ukraine and Georgia—but partly for reasons specific to certain countries.

Denmark experienced prolonged Russian hostility after it admitted Maskhadov's representative, Zakayev, to take part in a conference and then refused to extradite him. When Zakayev moved to Britain, Russia sought his extradition through the courts. Russia's argument that Zakayev was a terrorist was fatally undermined by the fact that, two years previously, a senior presidential representative had held talks with him at Sheremetievo airport—a meeting justified by the Kremlin on the grounds that Zakayev did not have blood on his hands. Shortly afterward, Boris Berezovsky, whom the Kremlin had forced into exile in 2000, successfully applied for political asylum in the UK. The Kremlin chose to retaliate against these two decisions, both of which had been dictated by UK and international law rather than politics.

Cooperation was withdrawn in certain areas. In the spring and summer of 2004, plainclothes Russian security officers forcibly raided the Moscow offices and several regional resource centers of the British Council, the official organization for cultural and educational interchange—an action without direct parallels even during the Cold War. From its apogee in 2003, the relationship between the Russian and British governments plunged to a nadir a year later—a surprising development, given the previously strong links between the two leaders and productive two-way business connections (the UK at this time was the largest foreign direct investor in Russia).

Germany remained Russia's closest ally in Western Europe, but concern began to surface in the Bundestag and the media about developments in Russia and about Chancellor Schröder's close friendship with the Russian president. This friendship brought a reward for Schröder when, on leaving office, he was appointed to a remunerative position on the board of Kremlin-directed Gazprom's North European Gas Pipeline company—a step that aroused controversy in Germany. Chancellor Angela Merkel used her first two visits to Russia to establish a more conventional style of diplomacy and a less uncritical tone. She gave due attention to Germany's substantial business interests in Russia, but without muffling her concern at aspects of current policy, and she chose to hold a meeting in Moscow, covered by the media, with a selection of independent political figures.

Institutional Relationship between the EU and Russia

Russia's formal relationship with the institutions of the EU is a curious mixture of detailed cooperation on very technical issues and rhetoric widely divorced from reality. Its documentary foundations are the (legally binding) Agreement on Partnership and Cooperation (PCA), which came into effect in 1997, and the less formal "Road Maps for the Four Common Spaces," adopted in May 2005.

These and other documents, such as the EU's Common Strategy of June 1999, embody the idea that the EU and Russia are seeking to "build a genuine strategic partnership, founded on common interests and shared values . . . in particular democracy, human rights, the rule of law, and market economy principles."[3] Indeed, the PCA went so far as to declare that such a partnership had been established and that "respect for democratic principles and human rights . . . underpins the internal and external policies of the parties and constitutes an essential element of partnership."[4]

The portentously named "Road Map for the Common Space of Freedom, Security and Justice" spelled out the principles underlying EU-Russia cooperation in greater detail, including "adherence to common values, notably to democracy and the rule of law as well as to their transparent, and effective application by independent judicial systems" and "respect for fundamental freedoms, including free and independent media."[5]

Beneath this deceptively ornate wrapping and notwithstanding a constant hum of each side grumbling about the obduracy of the other's bureaucracy, the EU and Russia have made a surprising amount of progress in dealing with the practicalities of life. As already noted, they

---

3 "EU-Russia Relations: Overview," European Commission, http://ec.europa.eu/comm/external_relations/russia/intro/index.htm.

4 "Agreement on Partnership and Cooperation," European Commission, http://ec.europa.eu/comm/external_relations/russia/pca_legal/title1.htm.

5 "15th EU-Russia Summit," Press release, European Commission, May 10, 2005, http://europa.eu.int/rapid/pressReleasesAction.do?reference=PRES/05/110&format=HTML&aged=0&language=EN&guiLanguage=en.

manage a large trading relationship, in which about 20 percent of the EU's energy comes from Russia[6] and 60 percent of Russia's foreign investment from the EU; they have succeeded in reaching agreement since 2000 on Russian accession to the WTO, the Kyoto Protocol, Kaliningrad, and other issues relating to the EU's enlargement as well as on many smaller items; and, without much fanfare, Russia has borrowed extensively from EU legislation on regulatory and commercial matters. The representatives of the European Council and Commission have an active dialogue with Russia at presidential, ministerial, and senior official levels, covering the main global issues. The joint participation of the EU and Russia in the Quartet on the issue of the Middle East is but one example. Recently this dialogue has been extended to include discussion of the areas of instability lying between the EU and Russia or elsewhere on Russia's borders and regular consultations on human rights.

It is not the case, therefore, that the two sides are failing to engage. But they are engaging while confusing their shared interests—which clearly exist—with common values—which equally clearly are lacking, and without a long-term vision of the relationship or a strategy for moving toward it. The Road Maps for the Four Common Spaces epitomize this problem. They have aptly been described as "an attempt to replace a strategic vision of Russia-EU relations with technocratic plans and cooperation between their administrative machineries,"[7] and as showing that "the EU and Russia are still in a state of profound mutual ambiguity."[8] In a surgical dissection of the 400 action points in the four spaces, Michael Emerson (a former European Commission representative in Moscow) has pointed out that the Common Economic Space fails to mention free trade even as a long-term objective; the Common Space of Freedom, Security, and Justice all but ignores democracy; and

---

6 The European Charter Secretariat signaled that Russia will provide the EU with around half its gas imports by 2020—some 250 billion cubic liters. This makes Russia the primary source for Europe's energy needs.

7 Sergey Karaganov, Timofei Bordachev, Vagif Guseinov, Fyodor Lukyanov, and Dmitry Suslov, "Russia-EU Relations: The Present Situation and Prospects," Working document no. 225 (Brussels: Center for European Policy Studies, July 2005).

8 Michael Emerson, "EU-Russia: Four Common Spaces and the Proliferation of the Fuzzy," Policy Brief no. 71 (Brussels: Center for European Policy Studies, May 2005).

the Common Space of External Security does not provide for joint crisis management in the areas of regional conflict adjacent to the EU and Russia but merely for "dialogue and cooperation." The Common Space of Research, Education, and Culture is the most practical because it is the least afflicted by political disagreement and provides for the inclusion of Russian students and researchers in EU programs and for common European norms for educational standards.[9]

The road maps, concludes Emerson, do not really inform us about where the EU and Russia are heading. This is because, at the moment, the EU and Russia do not have a heading. As an EU official put it to us, the main point about the road maps in the end was simply to get them signed off.

Underlying the lack of a reliable compass heading are the widening political rift, which we have described, and a cultural divide. On the Russian side, this manifests itself as an insistence on being treated by the EU as an equal, frustration at the non-negotiability of the *acquis communautaire*[10] and of mandates given to EU negotiators, and irritation with the EU's intricate bureaucracy. The Russians have a strong preference for dealing with the full panoply of 25 member states rather than merely the "troika" and for striking bilateral deals with the largest states as a means of circumventing agreed positions of the 25. The Russians are helped in this by the divisions within the EU that, over Russia, have widened with the accession of Eastern European states that suffered under Soviet rule. The differing attitudes of "new" and "old" Europe have made it harder for the collective institutions of the Council and the Commission to pursue a coherent approach.

---

9 The European Round Table of Industrialists notes that the Common Economic Space covers a wide range of policy areas and industry sectors, and that the major challenges within this broad agenda are prioritization and implementation. To this end, it sees a need for action to improve the investment climate; enforce intellectual, industrial, and commercial property rights; and boost trade and investment through elimination of unnecessary trade barriers, harmonization of technical standards and accounting and auditing rules, and a stronger policy dialogue. Rapid progress on such a formidable agenda seems improbable.

10 The *acquis communautaire* includes all the treaties, regulations, and directives passed by the European institutions as well as judgements laid down by the European Court of Justice.

For all of these reasons, the EU now appears to be marking time in its relations with Moscow, which is perhaps the most sensible attitude to take until Russia's course becomes clearer. The work program for 2006 and 2007 is modest. The two most significant items on the agenda are the energy relationship and the possible renewal or replacement of the 1997 PCA.

Russia's interruption of gas supplies to Ukraine, and through Ukraine to parts of the EU, in January 2006 had a shock effect on the EU, highlighting the extent to which the EU had become dependent on output from a source that no longer appeared reliable. Supplies to Georgia and Moldova were also interrupted (as had happened when Belarus was proving recalcitrant in 2004), and Russian politicians proclaimed their intention to use more widely the leverage offered by their position as a major energy exporter in a tight market. This was implicit, too, in President Putin's choice of energy security as the lead item for the G-8 summit agenda in July 2006. There had been growing nervousness in Western Europe about dependence on Russian energy, both because of the risk of political action and because Russia was being slow to develop reserves and struggling to sustain production growth. This nervousness was expressed to us by senior figures in Berlin and in the International Energy Agency well before the Russo-Ukrainian confrontation; and indeed the British prime minister had used the EU's Hampton Court summit in the autumn of 2005 to instigate a review of the EU's energy strategy. The dramatic events of January, at a time when energy prices were already very high because of events elsewhere, accentuated Western Europe's fears. They triggered an urgent debate about Europe's options and the need for diversification of energy sources, geographical origin, and transit routes. The European Commission's strategic review is to be completed in 2006 and is intended then to lead to an energy policy for Europe and a prioritized action plan.

The Ukrainian affair has changed the terms of the European debate on energy and has effectively torpedoed the concept, which some previously favored, of constructing EU-Russian relations on the foundation of an energy alliance. For years the EU had been trying to persuade Russia to join 46 other countries in ratifying the 1994 European Energy Charter Treaty and to sign a related Transit Protocol (whereby pipelines, including those under the monopoly control of Gazprom, would be open for transit by third-country suppliers). Russia's intervention in Ukraine ran directly counter to the thrust of the charter. Since then its position appears to have hardened against ratification. No progress was made on this key issue at the most recent EU-Russia summit at Sochi in May 2006. President Putin commented that "if our European partners expect that we will let them into the holy of holies of our economy—the energy sector—and let them in as they would like to be admitted, then we expect reciprocal steps in the most crucial and important areas for our development." How the EU's approach to Russian energy will be framed in its new policy has still to be determined. It remains the EU's aim to seek a comprehensive agreement with Russia covering all energy products and a contractual framework providing for the "integration of the EU and Russian energy markets in a mutually beneficial, reciprocal, transparent and non-discriminatory manner" (in the words of a joint paper by the Commission and the Council Secretariat). But in current circumstances this looks very hard to achieve.

The future of the PCA is a less pressing issue, but not an unimportant one, as the agreement provides the formal and legal basis for the EU-Russian relationship. The present agreement is due to expire in November 2007. It was negotiated in the early 1990s and signed in 1994, at a time when both the substance and the atmosphere of the relationship were very different from today's. It is a cumbersome document covering a vast number of sectors in fine technical detail and is therefore difficult to negotiate or renegotiate. Nor was it ever particularly appropriate, as it was modeled on treaties designed for potential members of the EU.

If the EU-Russian relationship was moving purposefully forward toward a deepening partnership, there would be a case for a new treaty of a much more ambitious kind, geared to the objective of a free trade agreement (following Russian accession to the WTO), and beyond that toward a higher form of strategic partnership or even a "strategic union." Some in Russia are arguing for such an agreement. The concept is attractive, but current circumstances are manifestly not conducive. The gap is too wide. There is too much uncertainty about the course Russia will take up to and beyond the 2008 presidential election—even about when the 13-year negotiation over WTO membership will finally be concluded. The objectives of Russia and the EU are not sufficiently aligned at this time.

We argue at the end of this chapter that the EU should articulate a clear vision of the future relationship with Russia; but signing yet another document that does not embody current realities, and thereby would fall quickly into disrepute, would not be the right way to do this. It appears in any case that the EU is approaching the subject circumspectly. The joint statement on the Sochi summit in May merely recorded that both sides "looked forward to the start of negotiations for a new agreement" and had meanwhile "agreed to allow the PCA to remain valid until a new agreement enters into force."[11]

Russia and NATO

Relations between Russia and NATO exist on two levels—the political and the technical—with little connection between them

Politically, the Russian government still treats NATO as an adversary. Russian politicians play on the negative image of NATO ingrained in the electorate, deliberately ignoring the fundamental reorientation of NATO since the Cold War. They suggest that NATO is seeking to encircle Russia, exaggerating and distorting NATO's liaison and training programs in the post-Soviet space. NATO's minimalist air defense arrangements covering the new member states in the Baltic have been presented in a menacing light for the benefit of Russian public opinion. The military doctrine of the Russian armed forces still envisages a potential threat from NATO.

At a technical and professional level, the attitude is different. Politicians and generals who in public decry NATO's enlargement say in private that they see no threat from NATO. Despite the military doctrine, defense chiefs have shifted forces from the western flank to the vulnerable southern borders. In private, the Russians acknowledge the logic of NATO's continuing existence as the world's only effective standing military alliance and an organization that can deploy forces rapidly to deal with both threats to security around the world and civil emergencies. And they profess themselves happy with cooperation in the NATO-Russia Council (NRC).

The NRC was set up with a fanfare in 2002 as one of the fruits of the new era of cooperation after September 11. It provided for an upgrading of the level, regularity, and scope of the cooperation between Russia and NATO established by the Founding Act of 1997. Its most

---

11 A fuller, meticulous review of the options is contained in Michael Emerson, Fabrizio Tassinari and Marius Vahl, "A New Agreement Between the EU and Russia: Why, What and When?" Policy Brief No. 103 (Brussels: Center for European Policy Studies, May 2006).

significant departure was that all members of the council (20 at the time) would convene as equals around the table—whereas previously the 19 members of NATO had coordinated positions before sitting down as 19 with (or against) the 1 of Russia. The NRC may not have fulfilled all of the ambitions that attended its birth and now has a relatively low profile, but it has proved to be a useful instrument. Russian participants regard it as successful, speak of a good atmosphere, and have valued it as a forum for discussion of issues like the Balkans, Afghanistan, Ukraine, and Georgia. Under the council's aegis there has been practical cooperation on terrorism, theater missile defense, the handling of nuclear accidents, and sea rescue; and there are plans to develop joint air-traffic control. Little of this features in the Russian media or political utterances.

Political attention is now focused on Ukraine, Georgia, and the forthcoming NATO summit in Riga in November 2006. The Riga summit could turn out to be as significant, or more so, for the future of Russia's external relations as the July summit of the G-8.

The Riga summit was not originally scheduled to take decisions on further enlargement. These were being reserved for the succeeding summit in 2008; however, the presidents of both Ukraine and Georgia are bidding for membership. Ukraine is already on the first rung of the ladder, having been accorded an "intensified dialogue" with NATO, and it is said to have made good progress on a technical level. The next rung would be a membership action plan (MAP), which sets an applicant on a track toward full membership some years later (assuming the necessary conditions are fulfilled). Georgia has yet to qualify for an intensified dialogue.

In terms of political evolution, neither Ukraine nor Georgia appears yet even to have approached the point where it would be sensible to advance to a MAP. Ukraine is in the midst of fraught negotiations, now in their third month, to form a coalition government. It has large problems of governance and economic management to address. The country's future orientation is under heated debate and will not be clear for some years, and there are many issues, including matters of territory and security, in dispute with Russia. Public support for NATO membership is weak: the most recent opinion poll (released by the Democratic Initiatives Foundation in Kiev on June 6, 2006) showed only 12 percent in favor of NATO membership and 64 percent against (as opposed to 44 percent in favor of EU accession).

Georgian accession looks even more problematic. Public support is greater, but the country is in a weak and unstable condition and under highly erratic leadership. Democracy is not firmly implanted. Corruption is rampant, and economic performance is low. Most seriously, as an unfortunate legacy of recent history, Georgia is embroiled in territorial and constitutional disputes over the regions of Abkhazia and South Ossetia, both of which have seceded de facto from rule by Tbilisi. Determining right and wrong in these frozen conflicts is not a simple or one-sided question.

Neither country therefore appears ready for a decision leading to membership. The wider dimensions of the decision also need to be considered with particular care. It is established principle that Russia does not exercise an effective veto over NATO membership and that NATO is ready to support the sovereign rights and legitimate aspirations of eligible countries. But this does not mean that it would be sensible for NATO to ignore the likely strategic consequences.

Ukraine's relationship with Russia is not yet mature or stable. The border is porous. The Russian Black Sea fleet is based, by agreement, in the Crimea—a region of Ukraine that is closely affiliated to Russia as, to a greater or lesser degree, is much of eastern Ukraine. Politically, for Russians, the attribution to NATO of such a large territory as Ukraine, which many of them considered (or still consider) to be part of their heartland, would be a seismic shock. The accession to NATO and the EU of the three small Baltic states, whose separate nationhood was more easily acknowledged by Russians, has played its part in the hardening of attitudes in Russia. The accession of Ukraine would have a far deeper and more lasting effect. It is not something for which the Russians are yet prepared. Although Georgia is small, Georgian accession would also represent a quantum leap in Russian eyes. It would implant NATO in an area—the Caucasus—of acute sensitivity (to not only the Russians) and, with Ukraine, would turn the Black Sea, traditionally seen by Russians as part of their backyard, into a sea almost encircled by NATO. The Georgians are viewed by the Russian public as having been aggressively provocative toward Russia and having given succor to the rebels in Chechnya. By no means all of these sentiments are rational or accurate. They are far from the only factor to be considered, but they are the perceptions or misperceptions that will shape Russian reactions, and NATO would be very foolish to ignore them.

Not for the first time, the Russians have been their own worst enemies in this affair. By continuing to paint NATO in dark colors, they have placed themselves in a position where Ukrainian accession would be seen as a huge defeat. Russia has yet to exorcise the ghost of a NATO that no longer exists, except in name. Russia's attempts to coerce Ukraine and Georgia have reinforced the arguments of proponents of their membership, especially in the United States and in some of the new, ex–Warsaw Pact NATO member countries. As a result, a lobby has developed to promote Georgia rapidly to the status of intensified dialogue and then to bring forward the previously envisaged timetable by granting both countries MAPs in November 2006 at Riga. In Moscow (notwithstanding the fact that Moscow's behavior would have helped to bring it about), this would be seen as the laying down of a gauntlet. For NATO, rational analysis suggests that the decision would be premature to the point of foolhardiness and would risk dragging the alliance onto treacherous terrain in a way it could well come to regret.

This is an occasion when the exercise of statesmanship is required. A decision that could do such incremental damage within Europe should not be governed by the simplistic argument that to do otherwise would be a betrayal of democracy in Ukraine and Georgia (the latter, especially, is very far from a beacon of democracy and the rule of law). There are many more appropriate ways of supporting democracy there and of helping these countries address their internal problems. Nor should it be dictated by the internal politics and electoral timetable of a member state far from the area, however powerful that state. Europe will be vitally affected, and Europe needs to find its voice.

Russia and the OSCE

There were hopes in Russia at the end of the Cold War that the Conference on Security and Cooperation in Europe, renamed the Organization for Security and Cooperation in Europe (OSCE) in 1994, would replace NATO as an organization to assure the continent's security. This never happened and, in practice, could not have happened. The OSCE is not backed by a military alliance, covers a wide range of 55 states of varying hues (several of them not in Europe but in Asia and North America), and lacks the coherence and muscle to function as a strong organization. At a less ambitious level, however, the OSCE has assisted with a wide range of problems thrown up by the sudden disappearance of the Soviet Union, focusing on conflict prevention, crisis management, and postconflict rehabilitation. It has provided a forum for sometimes fairly sharp debate about post–Cold War issues and tensions; is currently running field missions in 16 states (mainly in the

Balkans, Caucasus, and Central Asia but also including Moldova and Ukraine); and has done valuable work in monitoring elections, advising on democratic institutions, and defending the rights of national minorities and the freedom of the media.

Russia is the OSCE's second-largest member state, after the United States, and was clearly keen to make constructive use of the organization in the 1990s. In the more recent past, the Russian attitude has changed. It has been resistant to OSCE involvement in Chechnya and the North Caucasus although the conflicts and tensions there lie squarely within the organization's mandate and expertise, and the OSCE could have played a helpful and neutral role. The Russian government has reacted sharply to criticism by OSCE observers of the conduct of elections in Russia and has also been at odds with the OSCE's negative assessment of abuses of human rights in Belarus and the manipulation of the presidential election there. Within the councils of the OSCE, Russia's defensive and critical attitude now contrasts with the constructive approach of many of the other former states of the USSR, making consensus harder to achieve. Mirroring developments elsewhere, an opportunity for cooperation has sadly become a forum for empty polemics.

A further question has been raised in a recent report by the EU Institute for Security Studies:

> Which security should the OSCE guarantee—the security of the participating *states* or the security of the *people*? If security is state security, it has to be accepted that states are represented by regimes and their interests may be confined to the status quo. If it is a question of the security of the people, then the role of the OSCE should be different.[12]

The report puts its finger on a conflict of interest hard-wired by the Helsinki accords into the OSCE.

Russia and the Council of Europe

The atmosphere in the Council of Europe is even more polemical. The Council's main focus is on human rights, parliamentary democracy, and the rule of law. Founded in 1949, it is Europe's oldest political organization, but it had been overshadowed by the development of the

---

12 Pál Dunay, "The OSCE in Crisis," Chaillot Paper No. 88 (Paris: Institute for Security Studies, April 2006).

European Communities (now Union) until it gained a new lease of life with the end of the Cold War. It now has 46 member countries, nearly half of which (21) from Central and Eastern Europe. Russia gained membership in 1996 although not without debate as to whether its human rights record met the council's standards. It was an important step in the process of integrating Russia into European institutions. Russia will chair the Committee of Ministers of the council for the first time from May to October of 2006.

The principal body of the council is the Parliamentary Assembly, in which some 630 members of 46 national parliaments take part. Russia has been one of the most active participants in the Parliamentary Assembly over the past decade, clearly valuing its membership and sending strong delegations. The assembly's proceedings tend to receive much more attention in the Russian media than they do in Western Europe. Here, as in the OSCE, the Russian record, especially in Chechnya, has come under increasingly critical scrutiny. Because the debate is between parliamentarians rather than governments, it has often been vigorous and frank, free from the constraints of government positions and diplomatic language, to a point where Russian parliamentarians have at times threatened withdrawal or noncooperation.

The Council of Europe provides a test of Russia's willingness to correspond with the rules of democracy. Russia's position within the organization risks becoming increasingly controversial if present trends continue.

Russia and Europe: What Future?

As this chapter has shown, a Russo-European relationship for which high hopes were held and that has developed much substance (especially, but not only, in trade) has become fractious. The ambition on both sides for developing a genuine partnership has not so far materialized. There are further difficulties lying in wait..

Russian officials habitually complain about the double standards of their Western critics. With regard to the Europeans, they are correct—but they should ask themselves why it is that Europe views Russia in a different prism that applied to, say, China or the Middle East. Europeans have a strong desire to forge a partnership with Russia. They still believe that, over time, this is attainable, and they are frustrated that progress has been so slow. In a positive sense, they believe that the

European continent as a whole, including Russia, would benefit enormously from unification of their markets, cultures, and peoples—not in a single state, which is completely impracticable, but in a way that removed unnecessary barriers and established common standards while respecting national sovereignty, culture, language, and traditions. Such a partnership would enhance not only prosperity but stability. It would make conflict unthinkable. The alternative for Western and Central Europe of living forever alongside a Russia that rejects the idea of partnership and does not wish to conform with the norms of European behavior, especially if this is a Russia that relapses into weakness and instability, is not an attractive scenario.

There is another reason why Western Europeans tend to judge Russia against European values: these are the values the Russians themselves espouse, as President Putin and others have said repeatedly. Russia has chosen to subscribe to the democratic principles of the Council of Europe, reflected in numerous documents and agreements including the PCA and the four Common Spaces agreed with the EU. Russia should not be surprised or offended to be judged by these high standards, as are other European nations.

What are the prospects for moving closer to a real partnership? Could it, as some in both Russia and Western Europe argue, eventually take the form of Russian membership of the EU?

The current phase is a setback. We cannot expect a great leap forward in Russo-European partnership if Russia does not want this and while attitudes in Moscow remain as they are both to the building of democratic institutions within Russia and to the sovereignty of neighboring ex-Soviet states. There will need to be a change on both sides about the zero-sum mentality (examined further in chapters 8 and 9), a change in the predilection of some in the West always to take sides against Russia, and a change in the Russian mentality of seeing normal Western relations with CIS countries as a constriction of Russia's space and directed against Russia. The idea of partnership implies levels of trust and congruence of values that do not yet exist. For now, the substantial Russo-European relationship needs to focus on practical cooperation in the many discrete areas of shared interest. In time, this cooperation may help toward a convergence of values. Europe must not abandon values; it must abandon the pretense about values. Practical engagement is for now, strategic partnership is the hope for the future.

The EU's internal divisions undermine its effectiveness in formulating and implementing a coherent strategy toward Russia and its neighbors (several of whom are also neighbors of the EU and are embraced, rather uncomfortably, by its European Neighbourhood Policy). Solidarity over energy security is an obvious example. It would benefit the EU to make a more determined effort to bridge the gaps in analysis and coordination among the Commission, the Council, and the member states. It could also be helpful to have a stronger underpinning of policy advice from beyond the governmental circuit, linking the pockets of expertise that exist in policy institutes, political and academic circles, and business in different parts of the EU.

Looking much further ahead—20 or 30 years or more: Is Russian membership of the EU and NATO conceivable? In current circumstances it is so improbable that most observers are inclined to rule it out. They are wrong to do so.

No one can tell how both sides of the continent will change over the next generation. The European Economic Community had only six members 34 years ago. The European Union now has 25, with 2 countries due to join in 2007, 3 more identified as candidate countries, and 4 designated as potential candidates. Thirty-four years ago, indeed 20 years ago, the Soviet Union and the Warsaw Pact were still solidly in place; now they are 21 independent states. If such changes can happen in this brief timespan, who can say what might or might not happen in a similar period ahead? Were Ukraine and Belarus to become EU members, not to mention Turkey and all of the Balkan countries, and were Russia to meet the prescribed criteria (liberty, democracy, respect for human rights and fundamental freedoms, and the rule of law) and to apply, on what grounds would a European Union of over 30 states and around 600 million people reject Russia? Much the same could be said about NATO—an organization to which Russia could potentially make a very large contribution should it at some future time meet the necessary criteria and choose to make an application. Europe should not put itself in the position of asking Russia to conform with the rules of its clubs while insisting that it can never become a member.

The European Union needs to set out a positive long-term vision of the relationship it would like to develop with Russia. To declare, as some European leaders have done, that Russia can never join the EU but must forever be a "separate pole" in a multipolar world (whatever that may mean) is negative as well as unnecessary. The now defunct EU Common Strategy on Russia (of 1999) struck a more appropriate note, looking toward "Russia's return to its rightful place in the European family in a spirit of friendship, cooperation, fair accommodation of interests and on the foundations of shared values." The long-term vision should not be about membership per se because to raise such a question on the basis of current circumstances leads inevitably to the conclusion that at present membership is unthinkable. The EU (and NATO) will change; Russia will change; the surrounding environment will change; and the precise nature of the relationship—whether membership or some other arrangement—will need to be defined against these future circumstances.

7

Russia and Asia: Bilateral Ties and the Future of the Russian Far East

In sharp contrast to the impact felt in the European arena, the demise of the Soviet Union did not significantly alter Russia's geopolitical position in Asia. During the Soviet era, Pacific Asia constituted a major strategic arena for waging the Cold War against the United States. It was also a key consideration in Soviet efforts to guard against the People's Republic of China, a country with which the Soviet Union shared the longest national border in the world and that it generally considered to be a hostile neighbor.

During the final days of the Soviet Union, Mikhail Gorbachev made great strides in mending that confrontational relationship with China; thus, when Boris Yeltsin came to power in the early 1990s, Asia was no longer considered a priority for Russian foreign policy. Beginning in the middle of that decade, however, Yeltsin began looking once again toward the East, introducing a more geographically balanced worldview, which was subsequently adopted by his successor, Vladimir Putin.

In the early twenty-first century, Russian policy toward Pacific Asia appears to be shaped primarily by four major factors: (1) its relations with the West, (2) the growing importance of the Pacific Asia region as a whole and the rise of China in particular, (3) the rich endowment of energy resources in the eastern part of Russia, and (4) concerns regarding the future state of the Russian Far East (RFE).

First, Russia's policy toward Asia can be characterized as a balanced approach, a two-headed eagle looking simultaneously to the East and the West and behaving as a great power in a multipolar world; or it can be seen as "equidistance diplomacy." No matter how it is described, however, Russia's Asia policy reflects varying degrees of dissatisfaction or disillusionment with the West, and particularly with the dominant role of the United States in the post–Cold War world.

The priority for Russian diplomacy immediately after the collapse of the Soviet empire was the establishment of a partnership or even an alliance with the West. There were strong hopes that Russia would become a member of the "European House." Domestically, the major efforts carried out in the early 1990s under the presidency of Boris Yeltsin—particularly during the tenure of Prime Minister Yegor Gaidar and Foreign Minister Andrey Kozyrev—were concentrated on the historic transformation of the Soviet Empire into a Western Russia. However, a series of economic reform measures that were introduced at the strong urging of the West resulted in a sharp drop in production, hyperinflation, and ill-fated attempts at privatization. None of this served to create a positive image of the West among the Russian public.

Internationally, the end of the Cold War brought about a drastic compression of Soviet space on the western front. The Yeltsin regime was forced to confront the question of what sort of relations should be established with that post-Soviet space, which found its most poignant expression in the eastward expansion of NATO in the mid-1990s. In fact, it was the series of decisions to expand NATO to Central and Eastern European countries and to the Baltic states, together with the bombing of Kosovo, that prompted Yeltsin to assert the need for a multipolar world, as had been advocated by Foreign Minister Yevgeny Primakov (who replaced Andrei Kozyrev in 1996). As Yeltsin explained in April 1997: "Some are pushing toward a world with one center. We want the world to be multipolar, to have several focal points. These will form the basis for a new world order." Beginning in the mid-1990s, then, Russian leadership began to look to the East as a counterweight to relations with the West.

Second, the growing importance of Asia—particularly the rise of China—has been another decisive factor for Russia's balanced diplomacy. The Pacific Asian economy underwent a steady expansion in a pattern of development often called the flying-geese formation. Japan led the regional economy in the 1960s before being joined by the Asian newly industrialized economies (NIEs), the Association of Southeast Asian Nations (ASEAN), and finally China in the 1990s. Throughout the Cold War years, however, Russia failed to benefit from this most remarkable economic expansion. Now, Russia wants to change that and somehow climb on the Asian economic growth bandwagon. The concept of East Asian community building is being pursued with the so-called ASEAN + 3 (ASEAN plus Japan, China, and South Korea) countries at the core, and Russia wants to be involved as well.

The presumed major instrument of Russia's approach to Pacific Asia would be the provision of energy resources from the eastern part of Russia, which represents the third factor shaping Russia's Asia policy. While Russia's ambitions for becoming an energy superpower may provoke controversy both within Russia and internationally, there is no denying that, as the world's largest exporter of natural gas and the second-largest exporter of oil, Russia can be a major actor in the global energy field. In fact, Russian energy entrepreneurs are projecting a major increase in their sales, with as high as 30 percent of oil exports expected to go to the Asian market by 2020. Given the prospect of a huge increase in its demand for energy, China is naturally interested in access to those resources, but Japan, Korea, and Taiwan, being increasingly conscious of the danger of their overdependence on Middle East oil, are also looking toward the Russian energy supply with keen interest.

Fourth, Russia is seriously concerned about the future of the RFE. The fact that the supply of oil and gas will increasingly be coming from eastern Siberia and the RFE provides an important opportunity for the Russian government to engage in the development of that region, which has been suffering from serious levels of economic stagnation and a steady decline in its population.

Although the eastern part of Russia has not suffered the sort of "compression" witnessed in European Russia—that is, it has not lost its territory nor its zone of influence—the end of the Cold War has had a serious negative impact on the RFE as the region has lost the very sizable subsidies that Moscow had been providing to it for strategic reasons. Throughout the Cold War, Moscow had been completely sustaining the region, enabling the RFE to enjoy a standard of living similar to that in European Russia. Those days, however, have long passed, and the region has declined considerably since then.

The advent of Russian "energy diplomacy," which will expand energy supplies to Asia in large part by drawing on the resources of eastern Siberia and the RFE, opens up the prospect of long-awaited development in that region, if—and admittedly this is a big if—Moscow is prepared to do so.

How, then, are these four factors being reflected in Russia's relationships with the key actors in Pacific Asia? This chapter will focus first, and most extensively, on relations with China. This is in part because of the overwhelming importance that Moscow seems to attach to relations with its Southern neighbor, but also because this relationship has the most significant implications relative to all the policy factors referred to above. Relations with Japan, Korea, and India are then taken up individually. Although the latter is geographically part of South Asia rather than Pacific Asia, it is included here because of its traditionally close ties to Russia and because of the geopolitical significance of that relationship for all of Asia. Finally, Russia's future relationship with the Pacific Asia region in general will be discussed.

Russia and China

Having finally resolved the last of their long-standing border issues in October 2004, China and Russia improved their relations markedly in 2005, demonstrating an unprecedented level of cooperation: Presidents Vladimir Putin and Hu Jintao met four times during the year and issued a joint declaration on the twenty-first century world order; the two countries carried out their first joint military exercise in the East China Sea; and their bilateral trade increased more than 30 percent to $29 billion. Dialogue between the two governments also improved, as institutionalized consultations were held at all levels—from the prime ministers to ministers and senior officials—covering a wide range of fields from strategic security affairs to humanitarian exchanges.

Two major considerations underlie the new strategic partnership with China from the Russian perspective. The first is the change in Russia's relative position vis-à-vis China. Russia can no longer claim to be a big brother to its rising southern neighbor. Whereas the Soviet Union and China were still even in terms of their GDP in 1990, China's GDP in 2000 was three times larger than that of Russia, and in 2005 was four times larger. In fact, President Putin was the first Russian leader to publicly acknowledge the central challenge that a rising China poses for Russia. In a July 2000 visit to the RFE town of Blagoveshchensk, Putin commented, "If in the near future we do not make real efforts, even the indigenous Russian population in a few decades will speak mainly Japanese, Chinese, and Korean." It is commonly assumed, however, that what was foremost in his mind at the time was Chinese.

In this context, the Treaty on Good-Neighborliness, Friendship, and Cooperation, signed in 2001 by Putin and Jiang Zemin, codified the essential equality of the two states. Similarly, the historic settlement of the Sino-Russian border dispute mentioned above entailed Russia's agreement to a 50-50 formula on the three unsettled river island territories. This was presumed to reflect Putin's wish to foreclose any potential source of border disputes in the future, based on the assumption that time is on the side of China.

From the Russian perspective, another consideration in promoting a strategic cooperative partnership with China is the fact that the two have significant shared interests and common concerns on the international front. First and foremost, the two countries share an interest in ensuring a multipolar world as opposed to a unipolar world dominated by the United States. The Russians believe that their views tend to have more weight when supported by China, an idea that Yeltsin expressed as early as 1995, when he stated, "We can lean on China's shoulder in relations with the West. Then the West will come to treat Russia with greater respect." Also reflecting the two countries' common opposition to U.S. unilateralism is the fact that Russia and China are strong supporters of the United Nations and its Security Council. They emphasize the importance of maintaining established norms in the current international system.

Russia and China extend mutual support on specific issues related to national unity and territorial integrity: Russia opposes Taiwanese independence and recognizes Tibet as an inseparable part of China, while China endorses Russia's efforts in combating terrorist and separatist forces in Chechnya. The key phrase that they invoke is that they are cooperating in the fight against "international terrorism, national separatism, and religious extremism." Also of increasing relevance to both countries with respect to domestic governance is the recognition of the right of countries to choose their own development paths and their own manner of respecting universal human rights that reflects domestic conditions and traditions.

Central Asia and the Shanghai Cooperation Organization

Central Asia provides a notable case of Sino-Russian cooperation with profound geopolitical implications. With the demise of the Soviet Union, the five Central Asian states—Kazakhstan, Kyrgyzstan, Tajikistan, Turkmenistan, and Uzbekistan—gained independence. However, the legacies of commingled ethnic groups, convoluted borders inherited from the Soviet days, and emerging national identities have been challenging the stability of these countries.

At the same time, the geopolitical importance of the region at the center of the Eurasian continent—its rich endowment of oil and gas, its position as a major drug trafficking route from Afghanistan to points north and west, its potential threat as a host of Islamic radical terrorist movements, and the problematic issue of governance by authoritarian regimes—has attracted the attention of the major international players, each with its own respective interests and concerns.

For Russia, Central Asia is an important but difficult part of the "near abroad." Russia's relations with those former Soviet states have demonstrated varying degrees of closeness and complexity. In the late 1990s, Russia, China, and three of the Central Asian states signed the Treaty on Deepening Military Trust in Border Regions. That group formed the basis of an expanded Shanghai Cooperation Organization (SCO), created as an intergovernmental organization in 2001. Russia's interest in the SCO is primarily tied to ensuring the security of the region and preventing drug trafficking from Afghanistan. It also tries to use other post-Soviet mechanisms for binding Central Asian economies closer to Russia.

China, which shares borders with three Central Asian states, has had an interest in the consolidation of its borders to prevent incursions by Islamic extremists into Xinjiang Province. Its growing interest, however, is how to expand its economic stake in the region, and particularly its access to oil and gas resources around the Caspian Sea. (It already has a significant stake in a Kazakhstan oil field.) China therefore wishes to use the SCO as an instrument to promote economic cooperation with the region and has reportedly proposed the creation of a free trade agreement.

While Central Asia had been of interest to the United States for geopolitical reasons and for Caspian Sea oil, in which it already has a substantial stake, the events of September 11, 2001, turned the region into a critical strategic base for the country's Afghanistan operations. All Central Asian states granted overflight rights for the U.S.-led counterterrorism efforts in Afghanistan, and Kyrgyzstan and Uzbekistan provided air bases as well.

Japan has been a major aid donor in the region, with the amount of assistance reaching a total of ¥280 billion (more than $2.2 billion) from 1994 to 2004. As a major part of its Silk Road diplomacy, Japan initiated a Central Asia Plus Japan Dialogue with a view to promoting intraregional cooperation in such sectors as counterterrorism, drugs, land mines, health and medical care, water supply, energy, trade, and transportation. The first ministerial meeting, in which all five Central Asian states participated, took place in August 2004, and a second meeting is scheduled to be held in Tokyo in 2006. Japanese companies are also looking to the region, as seen in the participation by a Japanese oil firm in the development of the Kashagan oil field in Kazakhstan.

The year 2005, however, witnessed a radical change in the political landscape of Central Asia. In Kyrgyzstan, disputed elections led to a coup d'état in March 2005 that brought in new leadership. Two months later, there was a rebellion in the Uzbek city of Andijan, which the government of President Islam Karimov violently suppressed. Washington and Brussels demanded an independent investigation, which Karimov rejected. This series of events resulted in a radical shift in the foreign policy posture of Karimov, who prompted the SCO member countries to request that all of the coalition-force members submit a deadline for the withdrawal of their bases of operation from Central Asia. Uzbekistan specifically requested that the United States withdraw from the Karshi-Khanabad air base, which it did in November of that year. Presidents Putin and Karimov agreed to a mutual security pact that same month.

Given the geopolitical importance of the region, and the high stakes involved in the Caspian Sea oil and gas resources, what transpires in Central Asia over the coming years could have important ramifications for the major powers of the world.

Weapons, Oil, and Trade with China

With the collapse of the Soviet Union, the Russian military-industrial complex faced drastic cuts in the country's military budget and subsequently became increasingly dependent on exports as a source of income. As a result, it started looking to China as its most stable client. It is currently estimated that more than 50 percent of Russia's military production is being financed by exports, and China is the largest buyer with average annual purchases of well over $1 billion. Because the export of weapons from European manufacturers was prohibited as part of the sanctions imposed in the aftermath of the Tiananmen Square incident of 1989, the People's Liberation Army (PLA) has been exclusively equipped with Russian- or Soviet-made weapons. While the Russian side, cognizant of its own security, is said to be careful not to export the most sophisticated line of weaponry, the Chinese, with their increasing industrial capability, have grown insistent on obtaining more advanced systems and military technologies rather than simply purchasing items off the shelf. Thus, there has been an increasing number of cases of licensed production of advanced MiG and Sukhoi aircraft in China.

As China became a net importer of energy, Russian oil companies also started looking to the Chinese market. Until recently, virtually all Russian oil has been shipped westward, from western Siberia to Eastern and Western Europe. Originally, the Chinese market was also to be served by the western Siberian oil fields. The oil was first to be shipped eastward to the refinery town of Angarsk, near the city of Irkutsk. From there, a new pipeline was to be established that would extend to the Chinese oil town of Daqin via the southern end of Lake Baikal. However, a series of environmental impact studies concluded that the route was too dangerous because an oil spill would cause irreparable damage to the unique ecology of the lake. It was therefore decided to instead lay the pipeline from Taishet in the western part of the Irkutsk region, around the northern end of Lake Baikal, and on to Skovorodino, a town along the Trans-Siberian Railway to the north of China.

The Angarsk-Daqin route was originally contemplated by the Yukos Oil Company (headed by Mikhail Khodorkovsky), which intended to lay its own pipeline. That project was foiled by the virtual demise of Yukos in 2003. The Chinese who had enthusiastically welcomed the original deal were not happy at all with the changes, and they were further humiliated by a Russian decision in 2004 to extend the northern Lake Baikal route via Skovorodino to Russia's Pacific coast near Nakhodka. The decision to establish a trans-Siberian pipeline to the Pacific was thought to reflect the strong lobbying on the part of the Japanese government, which had long been interested in obtaining access to eastern Siberian oil.

The Russian government subsequently decided that, while the Siberian-Pacific pipeline project itself would be maintained for reasons of "national interest," the initial construction would start with the Taishet-to-Skovorodino portion, from which a connecting pipeline would be built by the Chinese to reach Taqing. It was also agreed that, pending the construction of the pipeline, China would receive a substantial amount of oil by rail. Apparently, the Russian side made a guarantee of long-term oil deliveries in exchange for a major loan from the Chinese.

If the contemplated pipeline is completed, its transport capacity will be 80 million tons of oil a year, of which 30 million tons would go to China and 50 million tons would be sent to the Pacific for shipment to Japan and other Pacific Rim countries. The question, however, is whether there will be a sufficient amount of oil. While the western Siberian oil field can provide 30 million, the rest will have to be explored, developed, and extracted from eastern Siberia, an area whose resources have not yet been tapped.

A second question is who will finance these projects. China and Japan have both shown an interest in buying into Russian oil companies. China has announced that it will make a substantial investment in "natural resource development," while Japan is reportedly prepared to provide substantial financing for both resource development and pipeline construction. Moreover, it is now estimated that at least 1.9 billion tons of oil are to be found off the shores of Sakhalin. Japan is investing more than $10 billion in the so-called Sakhalin I and Sakhalin II projects, which are joint ventures with Russian, American, and British firms. India has also joined in, while China has reportedly completed a contract with Russia for joint development of a Sakhalin III project.

Apart from discussion of the potential supply of oil and gas, however, Sino-Russian relations in the economic sphere to date have not matched the political ties. Trade continues so far to be dominated by border trade and weapons purchases, which amount to only about one-tenth of China's trade with the United States or Japan. Russia strongly wishes to expand trade relations with China not only in the energy sector, about which China is most enthusiastic, but also in the machinery and equipment sectors.

Although the low level of trade has been largely due to the plight of the Russian economy, particularly in the RFE, the Russian side is of the view that Russian products are being treated unfavorably compared with products of Western competitors. In the tender for generators and turbines for the Three Gorges hydroengineering project, for example, Russia lost to Western European competitors despite its lower bid. Complicating matters further, some Chinese companies operating in the Russian market are being accused of illegal activities and tax evasion.

In a November 2005 meeting with President Putin in Pusan, South Korea, on the occasion of the Asia-Pacific Economic Cooperation (APEC) summit meeting, President Hu Jintao emphasized that China would give top priority to expanding economic relations with Russia and pledged to take active measures to increase imports from Russia and make special efforts on cooperation in energy resources, electromechanics, and infrastructure construction.

Joint Military Exercise off Shandong Province

As noted above, in August 2005, Russia held a joint military exercise with China for the first time in history, the geopolitical implications of which are yet to be ascertained. It is reported that it took several rounds of negotiations to reach an agreement on the venue of operation. First, China suggested the use of a training zone in Primorskiy Krai, the farthest southeast region of Russia, which borders China and North Korea. The Russians rejected that proposal because the zone is being used for training against a possible Chinese attack. They instead suggested Xinjiang Province on China's western border with Central Asia, which the Chinese side rejected. China next suggested Zhejiang Province, not far from Taiwan. Russia rejected that idea as too sensitive and suggested a site further north. The two sides finally agreed to hold the exercises off the coast of Shandong Province.

"Peace Mission 2005," as it was called, officially purported to be a standard peacekeeping and counterterrorist exercise, but what was in fact carried out cannot be interpreted as a counterterrorist operation either in terms of its scale or content. The exercise involved nearly 10,000 soldiers—8,000 from the Chinese side and 1,800 from Russian side—and 140 naval vessels (including submarines and antisubmarine destroyers). Four strategic bombers and two cruise missile carriers took part from the Russian side.

The exercise was carried out ostensibly within the framework of the SCO, although it is certainly interesting to question whether a consultative body covering Central Asia could cover a naval operation in the Pacific. Observers were present from four of the SCO's Central Asian member countries as well as from SCO observer states including Mongolia, Iran, India, and Pakistan.

One possible interpretation of the exercise is that it presaged a PLA attack on Taiwan with the support of the Russian army and air force. Russian and Chinese spokespersons have repeatedly denied that theory, but exercises that included a blockade, forced air and sea landings, and the use of cruise missiles had unmistakable implications for Taiwan. Another suggestion is that the Russian government was keen not only to demonstrate to the West that it had alternative options but also to showcase military equipment to the Chinese forces. The Russian side was able to demonstrate its whole array of military merchandise. This theory makes sense given the increasing Chinese demand for more advanced military technologies rather than simple commodity purchases. And, in fact, it has been reported that a very sizable contract for weapons technology was signed in the aftermath of the exercises.

China and the Future of the Russian Far East

The population in the RFE region is 7 million and decreasing. This stands in stark contrast to the three provinces of Northeast China—Heilongjian, Jilin, and Liaoning—which have a combined population of 100 million and rising. The RFE has been widely noted for its weak infrastructure in the areas of transportation, communications, electricity, and port facilities, coupled with rampant crime and corruption. As noted earlier, the RFE was considered to be strategically important during the Cold War as a bulwark against not only U.S. forces in the Pacific but also China. The end of the Cold War, however, brought an end to Moscow's subsidies for the region. While the RFE has thriving lumber and marine products industries, an extremely high percentage of the operations are run illegally and thus the proceeds are not channeled into regional development projects.

In the early 1990s, a thriving border trade with China developed. However, the extremely disorderly nature of the transactions, with thousands of Chinese crossing the border and committing crimes, led Russian authorities to impose border controls in 1993, causing the trade figures to plummet. Nonetheless, border trade forms a major part of China-Russia trade, and a significant portion of Russia's arms exports to China are produced in the RFE.

The critical questions facing the region in the immediate future are whether the RFE can take advantage of the development of the eastern Siberian oil and gas fields that are now becoming a reality, and in what way Russia is going to relate this development to China. In other words, how will Russia define the Chinese role in the development of the RFE?

In reality, China already provides food and consumer goods to the region as a whole, making it difficult to conceptualize the RFE's future without China. However, Russia is concerned about China's potential to dominate the RFE; with tens of thousands of Chinese coming to settle in the region, the RFE may very well become a natural-resources colony of China. There is, it seems, a growing consensus among Russian elites that the issue of immigration control will be of crucial importance to the future of the RFE.

In fact, there are varying estimates concerning the number of Chinese actually living in Russia. The official number is 250,000, but a more realistic figure may be closer to a half million. (Exaggerating the number of illegal immigrants from China is a popular sport, with unsubstantiated figures of upward of two million being quoted, or claims that in every major town in the RFE there are 25,000 Chinese, or that another million Chinese are illegally coming and going between the two countries. Local wisdom has it that Chinese men love to marry Russian women and enjoy the freedom to have more than one child (which is not permitted in China) and that Russian women love to marry Chinese men because they do not drink as much as Russian men do.

Russia and Japan

Following China, Japan is the next most important element in Russia's Asian policy. For Japan, however, the Northern Territories issue—an enduring, negative legacy of Joseph Stalin—has consistently been the major obstacle in its relations with Russia.

The Northern Territories comprise four islands—Habomai, Shikotan, Kunashiri, and Etorofu—totaling 4,992 square miles. These islands were occupied by the Soviet army at the end of the Second World War. When Japan normalized relations with the Soviet Union in 1956, the latter agreed to transfer Habomai and Shikotan to Japan after a peace treaty was signed. At the height of the Cold War, however, the Soviets denied the very existence of a territorial problem with Japan. Gorbachev rectified that position when he visited Japan in 1991, and subsequent governments no longer deny the existence of the territorial issue. Yeltsin, during his presidency, had offered to resolve the issue by 2000, but he failed to pursue it partly because of his weakening health and, more important, because he faced strong resistance from the Russian foreign policy establishment. When Putin came to power at the turn of the century, there were high hopes in Japan that, given his power and authority, he would be able to overcome that resistance and find a solution.

The Russian position in essence maintains that the 1956 agreement should be upheld and that Russia should return just the two islands.

The Japanese position, on the other hand, has basically been that all four islands should be returned to Japan because historically and from the legal point of view they are Japan's inherent territory and were never Russian territory. The Shimoda Treaty of 1855 stipulated that the boundary between the two countries should lie north of Etorofu Island. Although both sides have in fact made serious efforts, a wide gap still exists between the countries' respective positions on the issue, and no solution is yet in sight.

In the meantime, Prime Minister Junichiro Koizumi and President Putin adopted a Japan-Russia action plan when Koizumi visited Moscow in January 2003. The plan is composed of six pillars:

- Deepening of political dialogue,
- Pursuit of peace treaty negotiations,
- Cooperation in the international arena,
- Cooperation in the trade and economic areas,
- Development of defense and security relations, and
- Advancement of cultural and interpersonal exchanges.

In the trade and investment field, the amount of exchange has been expanding steadily as the Russian economy has regained some momentum. Annual trade between the two countries is now on the order of roughly $10 billion, and Japanese manufacturing firms have started to invest in Russia. Perhaps symbolic of this approach toward the newly emerging Russian market was the establishment of a Toyota factory in the city of St. Petersburg in 2005.

Relations in the defense and security fields are also steadily developing with the exchange of visits of defense ministers and joint chiefs of staff. Joint exercises for search and rescue operations, as well as mutual visits by naval vessels, are now routinely taking place. Cooperation has also been advanced between security authorities on issues of international terrorism, illicit trade in narcotics and firearms, and international organized crime (including smuggling and illegal fishing). In recent years, bilateral consultations among maritime security authorities have been convened regularly, which is a remarkable development when one recalls that it was not so long ago that Soviet patrol boats were routinely harassing Japanese fishing vessels operating near the Four Northern Islands.

The most promising developments in Japan-Russia relations have been in the energy field. The Russian decision to construct the oil pipeline from Taishet in East Siberia to Perevoznaya on the Pacific Coast was welcomed in Japan, and concrete forms of cooperation are being studied by experts from both countries.

As noted previously, Japan is a major participant in both the Sakhalin I and II projects, investing in excess of $10 billion. In the next few years these projects will start producing oil and natural gas, which will be exported to Japan and elsewhere, including possibly China and Korea. If only for the sake of diversification of energy sources away from the Middle East, Japan is strongly interested in further strengthening cooperation with Russia for the development of eastern Siberia and the RFE.

An agreement, Basic Directions for Long-Term Cooperation between the Government of the Russian Federation and the Government of Japan in the Energy Sector, was signed on the occasion of President Putin's visit to Japan in November 2005. The agreement included initiatives for cooperation on oil, natural gas, electricity, energy efficiency and savings, and climate change.

Finally, on the issue of the Northern Territories, Japan and Russia have been exchanging formal and informal proposals, seeking to formulate a solution based on the common understanding—acknowledged by President Putin himself—that the unresolved territorial issue constitutes an obstacle to the further development of a constructive partnership. Meeting in Tokyo in November 2005, Koizumi and Putin confirmed their common view that both countries would continue to make their utmost efforts to find a solution that would be acceptable to both Japan and Russia on the basis of past agreements and documents.

There have been some noticeable signs recently of a hardening of the Russian position on the legal status of the islands. In September 2005, for example, in a live television broadcast, Putin said, "They [the four islands] are under the sovereignty of the Russian Federation. This is fixed by international law. This is a result of the Second World War. We will not discuss this point." This rigid position has since been reiterated by high-ranking officials of the Russian government. This change of negotiating profile might possibly be a reflection of Russia's growing confidence in its economic strength, its decreasing dependence on foreign capital, and its ambition to behave as an energy superpower. The rising sense of nationalism that is being expressed against the West in general might also be prompting the Russian government to take a stronger posture vis-à-vis Japan on a territorial issue that is particularly sensitive to nationalist sentiment.

On the whole, Japan-Russia relations are developing steadily on the basis of the action plan adopted in early 2003, and, as the Russian economy continues to forge ahead, further expansion of Japan's trade with and investment in Russia can be expected. Three issues are key for this relationship: the supply of oil and gas, the future development of the RFE region, and the resolution of the Northern Territories issue. The last is the most difficult, but from Japan's perspective it is politically imperative that genuine efforts be sustained on both sides to search for a mutually agreeable solution.

Finally, it seems hardly possible to overemphasize the significance of enhancing defense and security relations between the two countries in view of what seems to be a qualitative change in Sino-Russian defense cooperation. Improvements may be effected through the increasingly frequent mutual visits of high defense officials. In this area, as in others, Japan-Russia relations are gradually expanding, but there is still much room for improving the substance of the relationship.

Russia and the Korean Peninsula

When President Putin attended the G-8 Summit in Okinawa in the summer of 2000, he was at the center of attention, not only because he was the newly elected head of the Russian Federation but because prior to coming to Okinawa he had visited Pyongyang and was thus the only G-8 leader to have ever met Kim Jong-il. It was obvious that Putin wanted to mediate between Pyongyang and Washington. His attempt ended in failure, however, because Kim Jong-il publicly denied the promises he had privately made to Putin. Subsequently, Russia has had to be satisfied with being a member of the six-party talks rather than actively taking the initiative to help resolve the most critical issue affecting peace and security in East Asia.

Russia's rather passive attitude on Korean affairs in recent years seems to reflect the changing political landscape surrounding the Korean peninsula. First, due to the reconciliation between Seoul and Pyongyang, Russia no longer needs to be concerned about where to position itself between the two capitals, whereas in the past any favor or concession to either of the two would have invariably occasioned negative reactions from the other. Second, owing to its close strategic partnership with China, Russia need not be sensitive about the question of Pyongyang tilting toward Beijing, as has been the case in recent years. Actually, in the six-party talks, Moscow has consistently been supportive of Beijing's position.

On the nuclear issue, Russia as a nuclear power is against North Korea developing nuclear weapons capabilities, but at the same time it is aware that it lacks effective leverage to influence the North Korean leadership to return to the nonproliferation regime. What appears to be unique to the Russian position on this issue, however, is its reluctance to accept that North Korea's nuclear ambitions pose any immediate danger, despite Pyongyang's own declaration that it has become a nuclear power. Moscow cites the technical difficulties involved in developing nuclear warheads and mounting them on missiles and seems to be unwilling to acknowledge the imminence of a threat unless and until a nuclear explosion takes place and long-range missile tests are resumed. Moscow does seem to be putting pressure on Pyongyang not to execute either of those options.

Most likely, Moscow's seeming unwillingness to face reality is due to its reluctance to take decisively tough measures against Pyongyang, with which it wishes to maintain reasonably stable relations. It may also reflect a relatively relaxed attitude toward the danger that a North Korean nuclear weapons capability might pose to Russia's own security.

What concerns Russia most is the eventual emergence of a unified Korea. The collapse of the Kim Jong-il regime would affect Russia in terms of an inflow of refugees although the impact would presumably be much less than on China or South Korea. More important, however, is what sort of role a unified Korea might play in the geopolitical map of Northeast Asia. Given the inevitable uncertainties of such a development, Russia seems inclined to support the status quo of a divided Korea, thus making it a reluctant supporter of the Kim Jong-il regime on the assumption that, as long as Kim remains, there will be no reunification.

As a growing factor in the world economy, South Korea is considered by Russia to be a valuable economic partner, and the South Koreans are clearly interested in Russia as a source of energy resources and other raw materials. Following the normalization of diplomatic relations between Russia and South Korea in 1990, economic ties expanded gradually. The financial crises experienced in both countries in the mid- to late 1990s slowed that growth, but in the ensuing years it has picked up speed. South Korea has become a major trading partner, particularly with the RFE.

During a 2004 summit meeting in Moscow between Putin and the South Korean president, Roh Moo-hyun, the leaders pledged their commitment to a broad range of economic cooperation ranging from the energy industry to transportation, science and technology, the exploration of mineral resources, information and communications technology, and oceans and fisheries. Russia is currently assisting the South Korean space program, and negotiations are apparently under way on South Korea–Russia joint ventures in such fields as the production of satellite components.

Several initiatives are promoting trilateral economic cooperation among Russia, North Korea, and South Korea. The most notable is a project to connect the Trans-Siberian Railway to a trans-Korean rail line. This project not only would assist in the development of the RFE, improve Korean access to energy and other resources, and cut dramatically the delivery time for South Korean exports to Western Europe, but would also offer an opportunity for confidence building on the peninsula. Another area in which the two Koreas could potentially cooperate is related to the supply of natural gas from Siberia's Kovykta gas fields. China and South Korea have been in negotiations with Russia for the construction of a pipeline, and South Korea has reportedly asked North Korea to participate in the feasibility study.

Russia and India

Since the early years of the Cold War, India has consistently maintained friendly relations with Russia. India was strategically important in the days of the Sino-Soviet conflict, at which time India was considered by Russia to be a counterbalance to China, while Pakistan enjoyed close relations with China and the United States. As a result, India's decision to go nuclear did not antagonize the Soviet Union. India has long been one of the largest importers of Soviet and Russian arms and military technology, including very sophisticated weapons systems. Viewing India as a major factor in the emerging multipolar world, Putin has reinforced this traditional friendship by proposing to hold an annual bilateral summit and expand the scope of cooperation beyond the arms trade. Primakov's notion of a China-India-Russia tripartite cooperation scheme thus remains alive (although it has yet to be defined precisely), and such consultations are being held occasionally at the foreign minister level.

Together with Pakistan and Iran, India was invited as an observer to the SCO's summit in August 2005, held at Astana, Kazakhstan. India is keen to secure access to Russian energy to meet the needs of its growing economy, and Indian companies have taken stakes in projects such as Sakhalin I and II.

A new element of strategic significance is the rapid development of the U.S.-Indian relationship, which President George W. Bush referred to as a "strategic partnership" during his March 2006 visit to India. The visit dramatically demonstrated the thrust on the part of the United States to transform the nature of its relationship with India—the largest democracy in the world that also possesses outstanding software production capabilities—to one of a major trading partner. As a radical departure from a policy stance that had been characterized as cold and aloof, the United States announced that it was going to extend civil nuclear cooperation to countries that are not party to the Nuclear Non-Proliferation Treaty and will share important military technologies and capabilities that India wants. How this U.S. initiative affects Russia-India and China-India relations is a significant matter that will need to be closely followed.

Russia in Pacific Asia

While Russia has been associated with the ASEAN Regional Forum since its inception in 1994 and became a member of APEC in 1999, Russian relations with Southeast Asia have not been substantial. Throughout the discussions of East Asian community building, Russia has hardly been mentioned.

In December 2005, Russia held the first Russia-ASEAN dialogue summit and expressed interest in cooperating closely with East Asian community-building efforts. Russia, together with Australia, New Zealand, and India and the ASEAN + 3 countries (China, Japan, and Korea), was invited to attend the East Asian summit held in Kuala Lumpur.

A crucial factor shaping Russian policy toward Pacific Asia is Russia's need to promote the development of eastern Siberia and the

RFE—a critical issue given the current plight of those areas. The task is possible because these are regions richly endowed with natural resources, and particularly with oil and gas. Thus, cooperative relations with China are essential for two reasons. First, China is a neighbor with which Russia shares a more than 4,000-kilometer-long border; and, second, that neighbor's position in the region and on the global scene is rising rapidly.

The type of partnership that Russia establishes with China is of crucial importance. If the high price of energy is maintained, as many assume will be the case, those hitherto untapped energy resources in eastern Siberia should become exploitable if sufficient investment is forthcoming. Whether such a favorable investment climate will emerge in eastern Siberia and particularly in the RFE remains a question.

From the late 1980s to the early 1990s, there was a "Russian boom" among some Asian businesses occasioned by the very popular image of Gorbachev. Numerous small- and medium-sized Japanese enterprises entered the RFE to pursue joint ventures in lumber, marine products, and hotels, but almost all eventually withdrew because of the crime, corruption, and harassment by Russian authorities that they experienced there, coupled with a lack of legal recourse. There were apparent cases of collusion among local businesses, local authorities, and organized crime syndicates.

When President Putin came into power with the slogan of a "dictatorship of law" and the centralization of power in Moscow, it was expected that the crime situation, at least, would improve. Unfortunately, the situation remains essentially the same in many respects. Herein lies the crux of the problem: the task ahead is first to clean up the local security and governance systems and second to launch a comprehensive plan for the development of eastern Siberia and the RFE.

As was stated at the outset of this chapter, Russia has not been able to share the benefits of the remarkable economic development of East Asia. A major reason for this is that the RFE is not playing the role of an effective interface with Pacific Asia as it should. With the prospect of becoming an energy exporter to Asia, RFE should be able to develop a comprehensive regional plan in which not only China but also Japan, Korea—both South and North—and other Pacific Asian counties and the United States could participate with their respective capabilities. Japan for one would be interested in participating in such a development plan through investment, technology, and entrepreneurial resources. It is to be remembered in this connection, however, that persistent efforts should be pursued to find a mutually agreeable solution on the Northern Territories issue.

Finally, as if to underline the demographic plight of the RFE, Kamil Iskhakov, presidential envoy to the Far East, recently called for 18 million new settlers to his region from central Russia, ethnic Russians from the rest of the former Soviet Union, or residents of neighboring countries.[1] Although a target of 18 million newcomers to a region of, currently, fewer than 7 million people is manifestly unrealistic, Iskhakov's desperate appeal illustrates the plight of the RFE and the scale of the challenge it faces.

Future Shape of the Security Architecture

While remnants of the Cold War still remain in Pacific Asia in the form of a divided Korea, the Taiwan Strait issue, and the Northern Territories, perhaps the most significant change is the fact that Russia no longer is considered to be a threat to peace and security in the region.

Russia nevertheless remains a major military power with a nuclear capability comparable to the United States. If the August 2005 Sino-Russian joint military exercise in the East China Sea signified anything, it reminded Asian nations that Russian military forces are still present and functioning. If the joint exercise was intended to demonstrate to neighboring countries, as well as to the United States, that China and Russia have the capacity to balance the U.S. military presence in this part of the world, that would constitute a disturbing new factor affecting the regional security structure.

Although the North Korean nuclear issue is serious and has to be resolved as quickly as possible, one positive by-product has been the formation of the six-party talks, which demonstrate the common aspiration on the part of five of those parties to cooperate in maintaining peace and security in Northeast Asia. It would be unfortunate if this cooperative structure were to be adversely affected by Russia joining with China to form a counterweight to the U.S.-Japan and U.S.-Korea

---

1 Iskhakov is the former mayor of Kazan, capital city of Tatarstan, and he recently became the deputy head of a presidential working group to develop a state program on providing aid to voluntary migrants seeking to move to Russia from the other former Soviet Union countries.

alliances. With U.S.-China relations heading for stabilization (including on the Taiwan issue), this negative scenario appears unlikely to develop. The degradation of the Russian armed forces also militates against this scenario. Nonetheless, a word of caution might be in order. What is hoped will be gained from the six-party talks experience is the shared objective of the creation of a collective, multilateral consultative mechanism rather than the creation of a new strategic dichotomy.

That the rise of China has been the single most important geopolitical development in Pacific Asia since the end of the Cold War is not to be denied, and the peaceful nature of its development on the whole has been impressive. For that, China deserves praise and admiration.

However, there is a serious degree of uncertainty as to the future shape and conduct of this rapidly emerging power. A sense of concern is inevitable given that the rate of increase of China's defense expenditures has consistently exceeded that of its GDP—which in itself is among the highest in the world—and that there is a lack of transparency concerning the objectives and contents of that spending. How the major players of the world relate to this emerging power within this context will therefore affect the basic structure of peace and security in Pacific Asia. Accordingly, there is a compelling reason to believe that how Russia relates to China will have a profound effect on not only the future shape of the Pacific Asia security structure but also Russia's own security.

8

Russia's Direction: Toward the Main Highway of Human Development?

Substantial corrections will be required to the entire political agenda, which, multiplied by the astonishing ideology of building national capitalism in one country, is currently too reminiscent of the policies that led to the Soviet Union's disintegration. As it is, Russia is moving toward becoming a bigger version of Venezuela or Nigeria—oil-rich and dysfunctional—rather than toward becoming a great European or Eurasian power of the future.

—Sergei Karaganov
"Russia's Road to Isolation"
February 2005

Calling the current regime czarist does not mean that there is no difference between the Russia of 2005 and 1913, but it does mean that Russia is back on its historical path of development—roughly at the point where things started to go wrong—and has a chance of doing better this time . . . Russia is like Western Europe, in the sense that it will have to advance economically, socially, and politically by itself and in stages.

—Dmitri Trenin
"Reading Russia Right"
October 2005

Writing only 11 years ago, our predecessors concluded in the 1995 Trilateral Commission report that: "For the next ten, twenty or fifty years, Russia is likely to be in a state of greater or lesser turmoil." They declared that "economic stabilization is essential if the economy is not to collapse in a welter of hyperinflation. Social and political stabilization are essential if popular discontent is not to reach violent proportions." If the economy stabilized, they saw a reasonable prospect that, over the next generation or so, Russia would also establish viable and durable democratic institutions and practices. The most likely alternative was a move toward "mild authoritarianism"—some version of the Pinochet solution, elements of which were already present in 1995. Less optimistic scenarios included a growing lack of coherence between the center and the provinces and "a decline of both government and commerce into a swamp of corruption from which the country would find it hard to recover." More extreme scenarios of chaos or severe authoritarianism could not be entirely ruled out.

Broadly the same scenarios exist today. But, a decade later, the country and its economy are much more stable, and the most pessimistic scenarios have become less likely, though not yet impossible.

In this section of our report, against the background of the analysis in the preceding chapters, we seek to draw some conclusions about the direction in which Russia is heading. We look first at internal development and try to identify what obstacles still stand between Russia and (in Putin's phrase from his Millennium Statement) "the main highway of human development." Is Russia traveling toward that highway? What is needed if stabilization is to be turned into lasting stability, sustainable development, and a modern society, at ease with itself and the world? Second, we consider Russia's external relations and the direction of its foreign policy. Finally, we advance a view of the longer-term prospects. In our next and final chapter, we shall ask what approach to Russia should best be followed by the countries of the Trilateral area.

Russia Within: Direction and Impediments of Internal Development

George Kennan's words retain their resonance: "Give them time; let them be Russians; let them work out their internal problems in their own manner." Or, as a Russian commentator, Dmitri Trenin, wrote more recently, Russia, like Western Europe, "will have to advance economically, socially, and politically by itself and in stages."[1] A Western-inclined, liberal Russian businessman put it to us more bluntly: "The best thing the West can do now is to leave us alone; we'll work out our own problems."

It has become commonplace for Westerners to declare that Russia is heading in the "wrong" direction.[2] But Russians do not feel obliged to go in the direction that suits the West, and they have grown allergic to being told which way to go. "I am an avid supporter of developing relations with the West," said Mikhail Gorbachev on May 30, 2006, "but the West should not be telling Russia that it is headed in the wrong direction." Russians do not feel obliged to adopt a particular Western model of governance or to "restrain China in disagreements with the United States" or to adopt energy policies designed "to strengthen the energy security of the United States." Russians, like other people, will act in what they perceive to be their own interests.

It makes sense to start by asking whether Russia is heading in the direction that Russians want and that is in Russia's best interests. From the evidence of our contacts and of other sources, including opinion surveys, it would be reasonable to generalize that Russians broadly want stability, prosperity, to live in a "normal, civilized country," and to be treated with respect in the world and, especially, by their neighbors (in the latter case with deference to Russia as a regional power). By normal and civilized, they mean a country that develops into a modern state broadly approximating the norms and values of Europe, including the rule of law, social justice, democratic institutions, and respect for human rights but in a way that does not fetter Russian traditions and freedom of action. The social constriction of the mostly

---

1 Dmitri Trenin, "Reading Russia Right," Policy Brief no. 42 (Washington, D.C.: Carnegie Endowment for International Peace, October 2005), www.carnegieendowment.org/files/pb42.trenin.FINAL.pdf.

2 "Recent trends regrettably point toward a diminishing commitment to democratic freedoms and institutions. We will work to try to persuade the Russian Government to move forward, not backward, along freedom's path." See The National Security Strategy of the United States of America (Washington, D.C.: The White House, March 2006), 39, www.whitehouse.gov/nsc/nss/2006/nss2006.pdf. See also the report of a bipartisan task force, *Russia's Wrong Direction: What the United States Can and Should Do* (New York: Council on Foreign Relations, March 2006), www.cfr.org/content/publications/attachments/Russia_TaskForce.pdf.

highly regulated European states, such as Switzerland or Sweden, does not appeal to Russians and is seen as stifling.

Russians would not argue that these goals have yet been achieved. They would say that, after the mistakes and burdens of the past, the process of modernization is bound to take a long time. For them, too, it is therefore a question of direction. When President Putin was elected, he reflected and articulated his people's aspirations, and he took them in the direction they wanted. He banished fears that Russia might implode (fears that were strong in the 1990s and were reflected, for example, in the Trilateral Commission report of 1995) and took steps that were clearly necessary to make the country more orderly. The rapid development of the Russian economy, including the inflow of foreign investment, speaks for itself. The standard of living has risen enormously. To ordinary people, Russia is in most respects a much better country to live in than it was at the turn of the millennium, Russians have greater confidence about their future, and most of the foreign business community living there share that confidence. Any judgments about Russia must begin by recognizing the real achievements of the past six years.

Concern, however, is growing within Russia as well as outside about the direction of travel. This is not confined to the intelligentsia and to the educated elites, although they voice it strongly—in private. Opinion surveys have shown a widespread perception that the country is being governed ineffectively; that the hopes of five years ago that the leadership would achieve improvements in different areas have been replaced by disappointment and disillusionment at the subsequent performance; that trust in the leadership has sunk, as has support (on some accounts to less than 20 percent) for the handling of Chechnya; and that the fairly high levels of continuing support for the president are based on, as much as anything, the absence of a better alternative. The complaints tend to crystallize around three perceptions: that short-term, personal interests are driving those in power; that for reasons of self-preservation the administration has swung too far in the direction of control; and that events great and small have shown the governing bureaucracy to be as incompetent and ineffective as ever, and in no way improved.

There are four key areas—freedom, institution building, restructuring and economic and social reform, and the situation in the North Caucasus—in which short-term opportunism and heavy-handed control are cutting across Russia's progress along what President Putin has called the "main highway of human development" and raising concerns about the country's prospects for the medium and longer term. These are areas internal to Russia, on which Russians, not outsiders, will need to come to conclusions about what is in their long-term interests.

Freedom

Freedom is a term that needs to be used with care. It can take different forms. Freedom under the law is desirable; absolute freedom would be socially destructive. Freedom and democracy are frequently bracketed but are not the same. Freedom is a precursor to democracy and a necessary, but not a sufficient, condition for it.

Personal freedom in Russia was enlarged under President Gorbachev and widened hugely under President Yeltsin. The dismantling of the Communist Party of the Soviet Union and, especially, the discrediting and disempowering of the KGB after the 1991 coup were massive blows for freedom. Under Yeltsin, excesses occurred because many Russians took advantage of freedom combined with the weakness of law and law enforcement. To an extent this is still the case. Criminality still flourishes; the rules of the road are still flouted at will.

We have argued that personal freedom in most respects has not diminished under President Putin. It is inaccurate to label Russia as a country that is "not free." Most Russians live very freely and enjoy freedom of expression, information, belief, possessions, movement.

But we have two serious concerns, both of which have been expressed to us by many Russians. First, the political freedom of Russians is being constricted. The action taken against the administration's most conspicuous challengers has had a chilling effect. The impediments placed in the way of politicians and parties—of both the Left and the Right—not approved by the Kremlin have denied Russians the opportunity to hear and vote for a full range of political standpoints. Second, there has been a resurgence in the activity of the FSB and the other successor agencies to the KGB, operating outside the confines of law and accountability. Many different sources report that—in ways that cannot be justified in terms of crime or terrorism—the security organs have become more intrusive in the workplace, in places of education and training, in monitoring foreigners and Russians who have contact with them, and also in acting as an adjunct to certain business interests. Those who have been subject to the attentions of the security agencies speak of the return of the "fear factor." A not insignificant number of Russians have gone into exile for this reason.

Institution Building and the Road to Democracy

To speak of the de-democratization of Russia or of the rollback of democracy is misleading. Russia began to edge in a democratic direction under Gorbachev and during the first two to three years of Yeltsin's rule (culminating in the decision to hold direct elections for regional governors). But, as we noted in chapter 2, Yeltsin did not bequeath a democratic system to Putin. He talked the talk of democracy but in the end did not walk the walk, and the same is true today. There never was a golden age of democracy, or even democratization, to roll back.

This is hardly surprising. Russia needs to be viewed in context if realistic judgments are to be made. Democracy developed over hundreds of years in Western countries, through the transition from feudal sovereignty and collectivism to individual rights, including property rights. Russia has had only 15 years since Communism, and a bare 5 years since Putin brought in the first law allowing freehold ownership of land. The property-owning middle class in Russia is a very recent phenomenon. Russia's circumstances are quite different from those of Central and Eastern Europe (where rapid transition was possible in smaller countries with extant memories of a freer pre-Communist existence), let alone from those of Germany and Japan after wartime defeat razed the previous elites and institutions. Russia in 1991 was neither a defeated power nor a liberated nation. Its institutions and ruling elite remained in place, with a change of labels and abandonment of ideology. There was no alternative elite ready to take over, no surging democratic force in society (only a minority of enlightened liberals who were briefly given the tiller by Yeltsin), no consensus for radical change. Quite the reverse: one of the reasons for the resilience and cohesion of the Russian nation in the face of daunting challenges throughout its history has been its profound conservatism (epitomized by the Russian Orthodox Church, which, alone among the Christian churches of Europe, has never known reform and still guards its territory jealously and stands as a bastion against liberalism and modernity).

Russia had no sensible alternative to the evolutionary and gradualist approach that Putin espoused in his Millennium Statement. That is not to say that there is no alternative. The most likely alternative would be worse: populist authoritarian nationalism under demagogic

> At the end of Putin's second term, stability would be based not on the President himself, but on stable institutitons: a competitive market and democracy. This is Putin's mission in the next four years.
>
> —Sergei Markov
> Director, Institute of Political Studies
> *Moscow Times,* January 27, 2004

leadership, often described as a "Red-Brown coalition." It has suited Soviet and Russian leaders from Stalin onward to justify illiberal behavior as necessary in order to keep dark forces at bay, and there is evidence to suggest that the specter of an extreme nationalist takeover in Russia has been exaggerated. It would be foolish, though, to ignore the risk of populism and extremism in an immature democracy, should the circumstances arise.

The Russian leadership proclaims its adherence to democracy. It says, very reasonably, that it needs time to develop this and to find the right model for Russia. Stabilizing the country has been a higher priority. But an evolutionary approach needs forward movement. Without such movement, the argument that "Russia is not ready for full democracy" becomes a self-fulfilling prophecy. Nor is this a valid argument; there is plenty of evidence to suggest that—despite Russians' unhappy memories of the 1990s brand and their endorsement at the polls in 2003–04 of a stage-managed and strictly guided democracy—the Russian people want to move in a democratic direction and regret that they can no longer vote for their regional leaders. They want better democracy, not less democracy.

If, with the people's support, the leadership is to achieve its own objective, the authoritarian institutions and traditions inherited from the past (whether Soviet or czarist) need to be adapted and an environment created in which democracy can grow, as it has elsewhere, from the grass roots upward.

None of this is happening at present. There is no evolution and no sense of direction—only stasis and the consolidation of power by those who hold it. Political debate has been stifled. The Kremlin has asserted tighter control over the legislature, the judiciary, regional institutions, the commanding heights of business in the private as well as the public sector, the media, and civil society. This has happened not in circumstances of war or emergency but in the most benign environment Russia has known for decades. Far from promoting the organic growth of stable, independent institutions that would act as ballast and keel to the ship of state when it runs into choppy water, the Kremlin has enhanced Russia's dependence on a single institution—the presidency and the person of the president. Far from developing stability, it has accentuated vulnerability.

The presidential dependency is like a porcelain vase—hard and rigid and outwardly splendid, but brittle, fragile, and unable to bear a heavy load. It could last for a long time or break very quickly, depending on the pressures on it. The more that the presidency needs to shore up its position through authoritarian measures, which betray a sense of insecurity, the more it risks undermining its own legitimacy and authority. The question of legitimacy would arise in sharper form if the constitution were to be manipulated in the interests of an individual or faction, or if the next president were to lack the popular mandate that President Putin has enjoyed and be seen as merely the product of insider trading. The system is vulnerable because it stands on a very narrow base; because it lacks a mechanism for the orderly transfer of power from one leadership or ruling group or party to another; because the assertion of presidential control over the executive and the regions leaves the president dependent on the (unreformed) bureaucracy and responsible for anything that goes wrong; because there are no independent institutions to check and balance executive power, to criticize underperformance, or correct wrongdoing; and because there are no avenues for alternative viewpoints and creative debate.

In sum, Russia remains overdependent on a single institution, the presidency, as it was in the 1990s. It is not at present developing an effective, robust, and stable model of modern governance or promoting the growth of democratic institutions to meet Russia's needs in the twenty-first century, and it is therefore failing to move in the modernizing direction mapped out by the president.

President Putin once commented in his annual address in 2000 that "only a democratic state can ensure a balance of interests of personality and society, and combine private initiative with national tasks." The

Russian elite are acutely aware that their mono-institutional culture, frequently described as weak authoritarianism, is the "key obstacle preventing Russia from becoming a modern state," as one commentator put it. This awareness must carry the hope that, in time, a change of cast will bring a change of approach.

Restructuring and Economic and Social Reform

The Soviet Union collapsed, above all, because its economy failed. The basis of American power is that the United States has by far the world's largest economy. China's growing power is based on its fast-rising economy.

Since he first took office, President Putin has stressed to his fellow Russians the essential truth that Russia's position in the world as well as its capacity to deal effectively with its domestic challenges depend in large part on its ability to modernize its economy and achieve competitive success in the global marketplace. Modernization is not the only option for Russia, but the alternative—to remain primarily a producer of raw materials and semifinished products, with a shrinking population, importing knowledge and exporting human talent, and failing to integrate with the most advanced parts of the global economy—is not attractive to thinking Russians. Under this scenario, Russia's relative position on the world stage would continue to decline, as would its ability to influence events in its immediate neighborhood and, over time, to assure the security of its vast territory.

Modernizing the economy is therefore of central importance. In chapter 4, drawing on a large body of work by Russian and international experts and institutions, we analyzed in some detail the state of the economy and the challenges confronting policy makers. This leads to a number of conclusions:

- **Wealth has led to overconfidence, overindulgence and complacency.** The failure to press ahead with structural reform after 2003 is already having a negative impact on GDP growth, which is beginning to slow. Capacity constraints are affecting economic growth and are set to become an increasing problem.[3] Today's boom is masking deep structural flaws; trouble is building for the future.

---

3 Professor Yevgeniy Yasin has calculated that average annual growth of 7.3–7.4 percent could have been achieved at least until 2010 if policy had not changed in 2003.

- **A loosening of macroeconomic policy could be damaging.** The administration's laudable macroeconomic stringency has underpinned economic growth. It will be no less important in the period ahead to continue to manage the inflow of oil money and the appreciating ruble in a way that does not trigger renewed inflation.
- **The growing role of the state will undermine efficiency.** The size and powers of the bureaucracy are increasing, but not the quality and probity of regulation and administration. This imposes a high cost and impediment on the wealth-creating parts of the economy. The share of GDP owned by the state has increased significantly. This is not economically efficient, as the poor performance of state-owned energy companies compared with companies in private ownership has demonstrated. The future of Gazprom will be a benchmark of Russia's economic development. There is a negative correlation between increased state ownership and modernization of the economy.
- **Effective action is needed to combat corruption.** Corruption exists in every country. It is a global problem. It can be particularly acute in transitional and emerging economies, though not only there. Corruption permeated the Soviet system, mostly expressed in privileges and goods rather than money. It reached very high levels in Russia in the 1990s. In our research and our discussions in Moscow, we found a general perception that corruption has gone back up at least to the levels of the 1990s and is having a corrosive effect on governance and business as well as on the lives of ordinary people.

  A new campaign against corruption appears to be under way. A critical test will be whether action is taken selectively against those who have fallen into disfavor or whether action is applied without fear or favor across the board, under due process of law.

  Action in specific cases is a necessary beginning, but what will be required over time is a wider change of culture. One basic step would be to insist on measures to separate business from government at all levels and prevent the conflict of interest that commonly arises from officeholders, directly or through family or friends, having a stake in private businesses. It is also a curious anomaly that ministers and very senior officials should chair or sit on the boards of corporations. More generally, corruption and the abuse of office are made possible by the lack of accountability and weakness of those institutions—the judicial system, the police, parliamentary bodies, the Audit Chamber, regulatory authorities, and the media—that could expose and bear down on these problems.

- **Further and extensive structural reforms are essential to realize Russia's potential.** This is the view, overwhelmingly, of economists inside and outside Russia. The president appeared to recognize this when he warned in his 2006 annual address that the stated economic goals would not be met unless further actions were taken. Some processes of reform are continuing (for example, in the banking sector and in customs procedures), and there should be some beneficial impact from the national projects in health care, education, housing, and agriculture (which are essentially spending programs); but more fundamental changes are needed. The longer that action is delayed on steps to diversify the economy and make it more competitive—for example, on reform of the bureaucracy, demonopolization, creation of a fair legal environment for business, reform of education, health care, and social security—the higher will be the eventual cost to Russia.

  There is a pessimistic view that reform will resume only when the economy finds itself in trouble (as one businessperson put it: after three years of oil at $20 per barrel). It would be optimal to relaunch a reform program now, but a change of course seems improbable in the year and a half before federal elections. It must be hoped that the next administration will have the strength and determination to put the engine of modernization back into gear while the economic circumstances remain favorable and to preempt future decline.

In 2008 Russia's next president will face a vital strategic decision on whether or not to relaunch a program of structural reform. The magnitude and political difficulty of the task should not be understated. The policy challenges that we have identified here and in chapter 4 are daunting and will require courageous and far-sighted leadership. It will take many years to tackle social problems and the demographic crisis. Describing the agenda is far easier than holding the burden of responsibility for it.

The North Caucasus

The most immediate threat to Russia's security comes from the North Caucasus. The present conflict in Chechnya has lasted for six and a half years. The neighboring republics in the North Caucasus are also unstable and have seen outbreaks of violence, some but by no means all directly related to Chechnya. Instability in the region has generated acts of terrorism elsewhere. It should be of concern to all of Russia's international partners. Certain points need to be emphasized:

- **Chechnya lies within Russia's internationally recognized boundaries.** The Russian government has a duty and responsibility to ensure law and order there and to combat terrorism. The disagreement, both within Russia and outside, has been about the way the campaign has been conducted, not about the principle of countering terrorism.
- **At present there is no possibility of a comprehensive negotiated settlement on acceptable terms.** Whether such a possibility may have existed at an earlier stage is now academic. The rebellion is being led by extremists with whom one could no more negotiate than with Osama bin Laden. Western countries should be mindful of their own problems and lack of success in securing peace in other areas of intractable conflict such as Afghanistan, Iraq, and Palestine and should refrain from facile demands for a peaceful or a political solution. The conflict cannot be solved. It can, and should, be managed downwards.
- **There is a mountain of evidence that the security forces of Russia and of the local Chechen authorities have abused human rights and international humanitarian law throughout this conflict.** So have their opponents, but the ruthless and inhumane behavior of the separatists does not justify governmental forces lowering themselves to the level of lawless terrorists. That said, and without descending into a swamp of moral equivalence, it must be recognized that the record of other forces in similar situations, including in Iraq and Palestine, has been far from perfect. Maintaining restraint and legal standards in the face of civil insurgency and terrorism is a problem shared by others.

What should be done? Without underestimating the hugely difficult nexus of problems facing the Russian government in the volatile North Caucasus, we suggest that Russia:

- **Face facts.** Russia needs to face up to the fact that the strategy and methods pursued for the past six years—based above all on the use of force, and its execution by troops not trained to handle civil insurgency and low-intensity conflict—have not worked and that there is now an increasing risk of civil conflict in neighboring republics such as Dagestan and Kabardino-Balkaria. The strategy should be changed.

- **Develop a new approach.** A new, better coordinated, and much more broadly based approach should be developed, designed to:
  - Apply not just to Chechnya, but to the North Caucasus as a whole;
  - Preempt the escalation and endless continuation of conflict by adopting policies for the medium and longer term intended to tackle grievances, improve the well-being and social harmony of the population, and reduce the attractions of extremist violence and terrorism;
  - Address all aspects of the problem rather than rely solely on security mechanisms; for example:

    Use a minimum level of force by properly trained and disciplined security forces subject to the law,

    Develop political institutions,

    Develop fair and independent judicial institutions and law enforcement,

    Ensure civil and political rights, including mechanisms to combat ethnic discrimination,

    Work toward economic development, including a crackdown on corruption and fair allocation of economic resources and opportunities, and

    Deal with social issues such as education, health care, and housing;
  - Establish a single chain of command and direction, including control over resources, under high-level civilian leadership (current arrangements are fragmented).
- **Seek international support.** We believe that the international community would support such an approach and that Russia could gain by drawing more heavily on international cooperation, including within the framework of the OSCE. United Nations agencies and the EU are already providing substantial humanitarian and development assistance in the North Caucasus.

The approach we describe would not produce quick solutions. Regional stability, under any circumstances, will be precarious for years to come. We believe, however, that continuation of the current approach will lead to neither an improvement in the situation nor the eradication of terrorism and violence in and from the region, but is more likely to perpetuate and expand the conflict.

Russia Without: Direction of External Policy

The *National Security Strategy of the United States of America* issued in March 2006 warned Russia that "efforts to prevent democratic development at home and abroad will hamper the development of Russia's relations with the United States, Europe, and its neighbors." The Council on Foreign Relations task force, in its controversial report of March 2006, *Russia's Wrong Direction: What the United States Can and Should Do,* depicted a clash of interests between the United States and Russia over the Russian approach to neighboring states, the development of closer relations between Russia and China (which had "dangerous potential"), and what it saw as diverging responses to the threat of terrorism.

These are but two reflections of a growing perception that Russia has turned against the West, is pursuing an aggressive policy of opposing or obstructing Western interests in certain areas, and should no longer be regarded as a partner. The eviction of U.S. forces from Uzbekistan and the cutting off of gas supplies to and through Ukraine are seen as cases in point.

We should try to assess how this looks from Moscow. There is no question that the rhetoric of Russian policy makers has acquired a much harder edge and that the Kremlin has inspired vitriolic attacks on the West by television broadcasters. Why is this happening? Does assertiveness betoken aggression? Are there grounds for concern about an expanding Russian role in its neighborhood, in league with China and an assortment of dictatorial rulers? Is Russia becoming a natural-resources superpower? Is its foreign policy offensive or defensive?

The rhetoric has multiple causes. It appeals to a domestic audience that wants Russia to stand proud in the world and that sees NATO in a negative light (especially after the bombing of Serbia) and likewise the conflict in Iraq. Over half of Russia's population was weaned in the Cold War and regrets the loss of Soviet power. The rhetoric is a useful

> Last year, Russia began acting as the great power it had been in czarist times. Part of the reason is the country's much improved financial situation and the consolidation of power in the hands of the ruling circle. The humility of the post-Soviet period is now a thing of the past, Russian domestic politics is no one else's business, and Russian leaders enjoy playing hardball on the world field . . . No democratic and pro-Western czar will suddenly emerge from some color revolution to securely hitch his country to the US/EU wagon. On the other hand, Russia is not, and is not likely to become, a Soviet Union II. It is not a revanchist and imperialist aggressor bent on reabsorbing its former provinces . . . the West needs to calm down and take Russia for what it is—a major outside player that is neither an eternal foe nor an automatic friend.
>
> —Dmitri Trenin
> "The West and Russia: Paradigm Lost"

distraction from local problems—a means of transferring blame. At a policy level, it also reflects the disappointment of exaggerated expectations on Russia's part of the fruits of cooperation; frustration at loss of influence; and an overstatement of Russia's current strength. But, except in the minds of an irrational nationalist fringe, the rhetoric does not amount to an expansionist philosophy. From the perspective of Moscow (albeit not of Kiev or Tbilisi), Russian foreign policy is essentially a rearguard action, a matter of using such instruments and influence as Russia currently possesses to prevent further erosion of the country's position.

Russians are not alone in their national pride. For a decade beginning in 1991, they suffered the hurt of a dramatic loss of power and the humiliation of economic collapse. They had to tolerate patronizing treatment by the West and were frustrated by their sudden impotence. They struggled, and are still struggling, to come to terms with the realization that former satrapies and subject peoples were now independent sovereign states. Other metropolitan powers have faced a similar mental conflict, but none in recent times has lost power as suddenly as Russia. Experience elsewhere has shown the long process of establishing a new equilibrium between a former colony and the former ruler: the mark is nearer 50 years than 15. It should not be a cause for surprise that Russians are celebrating the end of their national humiliation, are indulging in a degree of hubris, and are keen to leverage wealth into restored influence and respect. This, too, is a phase in a long process.

Nor should the current mood simply be attributed to "cold warriors." There are of course people in Russia of the older generation, as there are in the West, who react to events with the knee-jerk reflexes of the Cold War. But this does not mean that Russians wish to return to the isolation and hostility of the Cold War. They aspire to be part of the world and to play a strong and independent role in it. And Russians of all ages, not just those who grew up in the Soviet Union, do not wish to live under Western diktat, least of all under the diktat of the American superpower. They resent Western criticism, especially where it appears to embody double standards or to overlook the West's own errors and failings (of which the imbroglio in Iraq stands to them as a prime example). This mood has not been discouraged by the Kremlin, but it is not simply the Kremlin's creation. It has gone very deep.

The first priority of Russia's external policy is Russia, not just in the conventional sense of ensuring national security—although that is a major headache for a country with instability along and across its southern flank—but also in terms of ensuring a strong foundation. The military power on which Soviet external policy was founded is largely gone and will not return. With a huge arsenal of warheads, strategic rocket forces, and nuclear submarines, Russia remains the number 2 nuclear power; and nuclear weapons will provide a guarantee of security against the growing military might of China or against any states in the Middle East that might acquire a nuclear capability. Nuclear status also gives Russia an important role to play in nonproliferation issues. In other respects, it is of limited value. Of much greater significance is the degradation of Russia's conventional capabilities.

Economic rather than military strength is the new underpinning of Russian power. It is undoubtedly the case that high oil prices, enhanced demand for Russian energy, the attractiveness of Russia as a destination for investment and a fast-growing market, and the spread of Russian corporations and capital into global markets have revived Russia's international position. They have given Russia soft power. Some in Russia have sought to parlay this into a harder-edged form of power, asserting that Russia could act as an energy superpower and could use energy supply, and in particular Gazprom's export monopoly, as a direct instrument of foreign policy. This approach suffers from some obvious limitations. The short-lived interruption of gas exports to Ukraine in January, and through Ukraine to Western Europe, undermined Russia's reputation as a reliable supplier and accelerated debate within the EU about the need to diversify energy supply and avoid overdependence on a single source. As with subsequent threats by Gazprom to divert exports away from the EU unless its demands for downstream participation were met, Russia's dependence on Europe as a market was exposed. Gazprom relies on Europe for its profits and—lacking either pipelines to Asia or LNG terminals—has neither routes nor markets to which to divert supplies for many years to come.

Russian foreign policy is officially described as multivectored. The most important vector is the immediate neighborhood, the area labeled as the "post-Soviet space." Policy in this area is not so much neoimperialist as postimperialist. Much as the Russians regret the demise of the Soviet Union, and especially the loss of Ukraine, Russian policy makers do not envisage the reincorporation of the former Soviet republics into the Russian Federation, with the possible exception of Belarus. But they see this area as their backyard, buffer zone, and zone of influence. To the extent possible, they wish to keep it within their orbit and oppose the gravitational pull of other powers. They have extensive and legitimate interests in these countries, including border security, migrant and expatriate populations, and a web of economic links. For most of the post-Soviet states, Russia remains the largest trading partner.

Through the prism of Moscow's zero-sum analysis, Russia's position in the backyard has deteriorated alarmingly over the past few years:

- **Efforts to build collective organizations have been conspicuously unsuccessful.** The Commonwealth of Independent States exists in name but barely in substance. Four of its members—Azerbaijan, Georgia, Moldova, and Ukraine—are forming a separate, Kiev-based organization, the Organization for Democracy and Economic Development. Ukraine has declined to become a full member of a Russia-led "single economic space" (also including Belarus and

Kazakhstan). Russian hopes are now pinned on the SCO, which includes China.

- **There is little left to play for in the three Baltic states.** The Baltic states' sovereignty, as EU and NATO members, is unassailable. They are a source of irritation about which Russia can do little.
- **Belarus is an awkward case.** It had no history of independent statehood before 1991. Ethnically, the Belarusians and Russians are very close. On paper, the two countries have agreed to a "union," and reunification would be popular with the Russian electorate, but the Russian government is in no hurry to assume responsibility for the backward economy of Belarus, and the country's erratic dictator, Anatoly Lukashenko, is an impossible bedfellow. There is no love lost between him and the Russian leadership, but the latter continues to support Lukashenko faute de mieux, fearing that any other democratic successor would take Belarus in a Westward direction toward the bright lights of the neighboring EU.
- **Ukraine is by far the biggest prize.** The Russians are striving to exert influence and recapture lost ground in Ukraine. The balance of forces in Ukraine over the next few years is hard to predict, but the determination of the Ukrainians to maintain their sovereignty and freedom of action was evident even under the Kuchma regime, and even more so since.
- **Moldova is problematic.** Moldova, with a stranded and recalcitrant Russian minority, is a problem and a small point of leverage rather than a prize.
- **Problems are ongoing in the Caucasus.** In the Caucasus, Russia has shown itself ready to coerce but not able to control Georgia, has a close relationship with Armenia that brings little value, and is less capable of manipulating oil-rich Azerbaijan.
- **In Central Asia, the situation is mixed.** Relations with Kazakhstan are amicable, but Nazarbayev is no puppet. Underpinned by a strong energy-based economy, Nazarbayev has built up Kazakhstan's sovereignty, skillfully balancing Russia and China, East and West, North and South. In Uzbekistan, as in Belarus, Russia is backing an unstable dictator for fear of the alternatives and must be concerned about the potential for future trouble and violence. Tajikistan is a poor country and a border problem that has leaned heavily on Russia; Kyrgyzstan is of little significance; and

Turkmenistan is under the thumb of a feudal potentate who deals on his own terms, has with impunity treated ethnic Russians roughly, and for the time being has to export his abundant gas through Russia's pipelines.

All in all, the post-Soviet space scarcely adds up to an enviable or easy set of relationships for Russia, still less to a twenty-first century recrudescence of the Great Game beloved by editorialists.

China is another vector. As noted in chapter 7, Sino-Russian relations are better than ever before. Contentious issues have been resolved, high-level visits are exchanged, and there have been much-trumpeted joint military exercises. This demonstrates, Russian diplomats say, that Russia can play the role of a Eurasian power and not be beholden to the West. A more accurate perception was recently quoted in the Chinese media: "hot on the top but cold on the bottom."

Russia's attitude to China is schizophrenic: a good friend, a major trading partner, potentially an important market for energy exports from Siberia and the Far East—but also (as Russian generals and strategists privately acknowledge) Russia's biggest long-term strategic concern. Russia is in an uncomfortable position: Russia supplies advanced weapons technology to a neighbor and rival that has far outstripped it economically and is set to become a much more substantial military and global power in the course of the next generation, and Russia also possesses a storehouse of raw materials in its underpopulated and depopulating Siberian and Far Eastern provinces, adjacent to overpopulated, resource-hungry China. Becoming China's junior partner does not attract Russia, and the Russians are also aware that, outside the area of defense, China has much more substantial (if more fractious) relationships with others, including trade with the United States that is 10 times the volume of Sino-Russian trade. It is a strategic partnership with considerable limitations and constraints, and it is a big question mark over Russia's long-term future.

The other important vectors of Russian foreign policy, which we have also examined in previous chapters, are with the United States and the EU. (Lesser vectors include India, a big trade partner and the second-largest market for defense exports; APEC, and the Middle East.) For all the talk of energy leverage and the rebarbative rhetoric we have noted above, Russia has gone to considerable lengths to avoid, thus far, renewed confrontation on any issue of prime importance to the United States (more by accident than design, Russia found itself an adjunct to the Franco-German *front de refus* over Iraq but in our view would not have cast a lone veto). Although relations with the EU are frequently testy, the EU is by far Russia's largest trading partner and source of foreign investment, which is both a very positive element and a mutual constraint.

Our broad conclusion is that Russia's external policy has certainly become more assertive as Russia has regained strength and confidence, but Russia is essentially defensive and independent rather than aggressive and expansionist. Russia will use pressure of many kinds on less powerful neighboring states and use leverage with the major powers where it has it (Russian diplomacy over Iran being a prime example), but it does not seek confrontation with them. Russia's leaders seem largely indifferent to the damage that actions such as the Yukos affair, the abuse of human rights in Chechnya, or the bullying of Ukraine and Georgia have done to Russia's image abroad. For the time being, Russia is not ready to accept the constraints on behavior at home and abroad that would lead to a closer partnership with the Trilateral countries. The trend is in a different direction: the ambition of the present leadership, supported by the majority of the electorate, is to reestablish Russia as a strong, independent, and unfettered actor on the global stage.

Beyond 2008: The Longer-Term Prospects

The Russian transition is too complex and profound for it ever to have been a neatly linear progression. The present order in Russia, like the Yeltsin administration of the 1990s, is a phase in the transition, not the final destination. How long this phase will last, no one can say. Unless the group now in power changes course, what lies ahead are more difficult times, which different approaches could have preempted or mitigated. The absence of strong and differentiated institutions providing for the representation of diverse views is not a model for long-term stability. The lack of diversification and fair competition in business is not a model for an advanced, sustainable economy. The postponement of structural reform in the social services, combined with widening disparity of incomes, is not a model for social harmony. After the intoxication with wealth will come a sobering up.

But what thereafter? Russia will not go down the same path of economic development as China and India because its economy is of a totally different nature: high on resources but low on population. China

> Russia is one of world history's great survivors. It has been in desperate situations—and it has recovered from them, even in some respects thrived. Its society and culture are extraordinarily resilient. It will, though, need statesmen of unusual ability and vision, not only to bring about change but also to rescue what was valuable in its past and remold it in a form viable for the twenty-first century.
>
> —Geoffrey Hosking
> *Russia and the Russians: A History,* 2001.

and India are on the rise, with new industries developing, investment in research and development accelerating (in China's case by about 25 percent a year), competitiveness improving, and national power and influence increasing. Russia is in the opposite situation: needing to revitalize a once-great (but defense-oriented) scientific and technological research base in which investment has fallen away, needing to modernize an uncompetitive primary product–based economy, and struggling to shore up its historic position as a major power. If Russia is to be more than an exporter of primary products, and perhaps over time to become a more closely connected member of the European family, a huge amount will depend on its ability to reinvigorate historic strengths in education and research and apply them to the development of knowledge-based industries and services within an open market economy.

Unless Russia succeeds in modernization and keeps pace with rapid change elsewhere, it will risk losing relevance in a fast-developing world and thus will fail to take the place in the sun that the Goldman Sachs BRIC projection assigned to it.

Over the coming generation, Russia faces a clash of cultures. Some wish to assert Russian identity through political and economic protectionism; state control; and preservation of the country's traditional, conservative, and authoritarian model of governance and reject external values. Others (no less strongly) look to their national pride to lead them in the opposite direction, toward proving that Russia can modernize, compete, and join the world's advanced economies by taking advantage of models of best practices elsewhere.

This is Russia's choice. The Russian people will need to decide for themselves what sort of future they want for their country. The current leadership started on a reformist and modernizing course but, cushioned by wealth, has reverted to the former, traditional model. This model, unless it is changed, will lead toward stagnation, rising dissatisfaction at bad governance and at backward public services, and an underperforming economy, which will become increasingly uncompetitive and inefficient in the sectors now seized and occupied by the state.

The first reaction, whenever it comes, will not necessarily be a swing back toward modernization. If the economy declines or if Russia is subjected to other internal or external shocks, power could be taken by retrogressive nationalists of a more extreme kind.

Over time, however, there is a prospect of modernizing business-led evolution (not revolution) in Russia. For the time being, senior Russian businesspeople are keeping their heads down and aligning with those in power, preferring to work comfortably from within rather than vulnerably from without. Younger educated Russians are concentrating on making money and enjoying the material rewards, almost ignoring politics so long as there is no intrusion on their lifestyles. This is the short term picture. But business is not static. Highly capable new business leaders, untainted by the 1990s, are beginning to emerge. Business and finance are attracting the most talented members of the coming generation—young professionals whose abilities compare with the best to be found anywhere in the world. In the areas that are not overshadowed by the state, some successful companies are emerging and are beginning to compete beyond Russia's boundaries. These businesses interact with advanced sectors of the global economy and are ineluctably importing its knowledge and practices into Russia. The contrast between commercially run, competitive businesses and old-style, value-extracting, state-subsidized industries will become increasingly sharp as Russia necessarily relearns some of the painful lessons of the past.

The potential clearly exists for business to act as the most dynamic force for change over the next generation if, in the competition for ascendancy between the old and new cultures, modernity is not defeated by unreconstructed conservatism. So does the potential for Russia to move at its own pace and in its own way toward more democratic institutions, although this is far from the only scenario. There are many positive forces in Russia, including the effect of travel and a quantum leap in the spread of information. The first genuinely post-Soviet gen-

> Another generation may melt these extremes into a more consistent mass. The Russians may one day become what we now are and, notwithstanding our present boasted superiority, we may possibly relapse into that barbarism from which they are endeavoring to emerge.
>
> —Sir George Macartney
> *An Account of Russia,* 1768

eration of leaders and managers will rise incrementally into the top positions over the next 15 to 20 years. This generation was not brought up in the Soviet value system and will not wish to be cut off from the mainstream of international society and the global economy. This generation will be no less proud than its forebears of Russia's history, traditions, and distinctiveness. But it will probably seek to meld into Russia's fabric the values and systems—the rule of law, civil and political rights, and democratic institutions—that have worked for modern societies elsewhere.

9

How Should the Trilateral Countries Respond? Strategic Partnership or Pragmatic Engagement?

> The West needs to adopt an issue-based approach when dealing with the Russian government, but it should not expect Moscow to follow its lead. Engaging Russia is over; engaging with Russia, where possible and desirable, will be based on mutual self-interest.
>
> —Dmitri Trenin
> "The West and Russia: Paradigm Lost"

In various ways, the states of the Trilateral area have signed up to "partnership" with Russia—collectively through bodies like the G-8, the EU and APEC, and in a host of bilateral documents and statements. With great relief they moved Russia from the list of problems on the agenda to the list of partners around the table. They welcomed President Putin's intention to stabilize and modernize Russia, integrate it more closely into the international system and fellowship, and be an ally in the struggle against terrorism. If the present trend in Russia is now heading in a different direction, if Russia for the time being does not wish to accept the constraints of partnership, a different approach is needed. We have important business to conduct with Russia. We should not abandon the long-term goal of partnership. But we have to deal with Russia as it is, not as we might ideally wish it to be.

This final chapter of our report looks first at the general and conceptual approach to Russia; then at certain specific issues of policy; and finally at instruments of engagement.

General and Conceptual Approach

Act with patience and understanding. There remains a gulf of ignorance between Russia and the world around. With regard to Russian policy makers, Sergei Karaganov has complained that "our knowledge and understanding of the rest of the world continues to deteriorate."[1] Much the same could be said of the Trilateral area, where the attention paid to Russia has declined markedly since the early 1990s. If we view Russia solely through a Western prism, we shall not reach the right conclusions. The current exasperation with Russia stems in part from a failure to appreciate the scale of the task. We need a more realistic understanding of Russian attitudes, of what is achievable, and of the time it will take. Russia has a 70-year gap in its political, social, and economic development to make up. We also need to understand the limits to the ability of outsiders to influence events within Russia. The Trilateral countries are not entirely without influence, but they cannot impose their point of view; attempts to do so tend to be counterproductive. Change will come from within, and the outside world will need to wait for events to unfold. This is not an argument for being mealymouthed. It is an argument for being realistic.

Stand by our principles . . . Part of our patient approach must be to be clear about our principles and stand by them. This is crucial to those in Russia who wish to move their country toward similar principles. Values are in no sense irrelevant to the debate. The dichotomy that some would draw between values and interests is false because promoting (not imposing) recognized values is an important interest and can enhance stability. The Russian state has subscribed to the values embraced by the United Nations Charter, the Universal Declaration of Human Rights, the Helsinki Final Act, and the Council of Europe. President Putin has declared that "the ideals of freedom, human rights, justice and democracy" are Russia's "determining values."[2] The Helsinki Final Act became both a beacon and a yardstick in the Soviet Union. Trilateral states should continue to show where they stand, and not give an impression that they are blind to dereliction of values.

---

1 Sergei Karaganov, "Russia's Road to Isolation," *Project Syndicate*, February 2005, www.project-syndicate.org/commentary/karaganov10.

2 Vladimir V. Putin, address to the Federal Assembly, April 25, 2005.

> Russia has been one of the great survivors of history. With luck she will resume her erratic journey towards democracy and pluralism. We are not, however, doing much to encourage this process, conniving rather at policies and attitudes that will encourage a more dangerous neighbourhood for us all. Russia needs a strong and outspoken partner in Europe, not a mealy-mouthed pushover. If we want Russia to share our values, a good place to start standing up for them is in Russia herself.
>
> —Chris Patten
> *Not Quite the Diplomat,* 2005

. . . but avoid megaphone diplomacy, zero-sum approaches, and double standards. What we say is important. How we say it—and who says it, and even where it is said—is also important. Russian hard-liners like nothing better than Western attacks that they can depict as threatening, as showing a desire to weaken Russia, or as betraying double standards. Name-calling on both sides can play well with sections of domestic opinion but becomes an escalating and counterproductive process that does nothing to advance policy and undermines the advocates of moderation and sensible engagement.

Develop a consistent approach and a long-term vision. There has been a tendency for policy in Trilateral countries to lurch from euphoria to despair, from engagement to disengagement, from attention to inattention. We need to anchor policy with a long-term vision of the sort of relationship we are offering and seeking to build with Russia, a vision that looks well beyond the next half decade or presidential term. Three points should be articulated very clearly:

- **We want Russia to be strong, prosperous and successful, not weak, divided, unstable, and poor.** We have no argument with the Russian leadership's aim to build a strong state in the terms in which they define this: that is, a state founded on economic, not

> We have reached a limit in political conservative evolution. If we cross this line, we will give the "knights and pawns" of the Cold War in the West an excuse for worsening relations with Russia. These people feel lost; they cannot live without an enemy, nor are they able to acknowledge past mistakes. They will be playing into the hand of our own "knights and pawns" who, driven by their parochial mentality and old stereotypes, would like to fight against America, not fight for Russia, pushing the country into ruinous isolationism. We cannot allow the creation of an "unholy alliance" of the most backward elements within our policy-making class. They or their predecessors, have already caused us colossal damage by playing into each other's hands during the real Cold War.
>
> —Sergei Karaganov
> "Russia-U.S.: Back to Peaceful Coexistence?"
> *Rossiyskaya Gazeta,* March 24, 2006

military, might. There is no substance to suggestions by certain Russian politicians that Western countries are trying to weaken Russia. This smacks of Cold War paranoia and is irrational to the point of absurdity. From an external perspective, the most threatening situation would be a weak and unstable Russia in which extremist elements might come to the fore, the security of stockpiles of weapons of mass destruction could be jeopardized, localized conflicts could ignite, and Russia would become a much less reliable source of energy and other raw materials. A strong Russia has the capacity to make a large contribution to global stability and the global economy. The more the Russian economy develops, the more important Russia will become as a partner in trade and investment—in both directions.

- **Strong, independent neighbors would be to Russia's advantage, not disadvantage.** Russia's strength should not be and need not be at the expense of the neighboring ex-Soviet countries. It will not benefit Russia to have weak and unstable countries on its borders. The successful development of these countries, and the evolution of a mature relationship between them and the former metropolitan power as sovereign states, will be mutually beneficial and will undoubtedly be good for Russian security and Russian trade. It follows that for Trilateral countries to develop close and supportive relationships simultaneously with Russia and with other post-Soviet states should imply no conflict of interest.
- **There should be no dividing lines, no closed doors, and no exceptionalism.** Russia should be treated according to its merits and judged by its actions—not by negative emotions from the past, nor by wishful thinking about the future. International associations and relationships should be open to Russia on the same basis as to others, and Russia should abide by the same rules as others. The EU and NATO should make very clear that they have no intention of drawing a new dividing line within the European continent, from the eastern end of the Baltic to the Black Sea; that it remains their aspiration to create a Europe whole and free, within which people and goods can travel freely and securely; and that they recognize the Russian people as part of the European family of nations. It is important to signal to the Russians that the doors are open to them and that there is no intention of treating them as second-class or alien inhabitants of the shared continent. None of this requires decisions to be taken at this stage on the hypothetical questions of Russian membership of the EU or NATO; At present Russia is neither qualified for membership, nor is it seeking it. It may choose never to do so, but there is no need to exclude any possibility for a future that we cannot accurately predict, and no sense in doing so.

Define the relationship honestly. Strategic partnership or pragmatic engagement? The many proclamations of a "strategic partnership based on common values and shared interests" were premature and have acquired a hollow sound. Strategic partnership is a worthy aspiration, but it has become no more than a slogan. To talk in these terms before we can make it a reality debases the language of diplomacy. At present neither Russia nor the Trilateral area (or countries within it) is ready to form a genuine partnership on terms acceptable to the other. We should acknowledge this fact without undue rancor or name-calling, cease to use the term strategic partnership, and find a more honest way of defining the relationship. This would help to limit the mood swings and acrimony that deceptive terminology engenders.

In practice, grandiose, baroque concepts such as strategic partnership do nothing to enhance relations or affect the agenda of day-to-day business. A partnership, like democracy, has to be built from the ground up. At its core is the idea that support will be given and received in the interests of advancing a common cause, not simply traded against countervailing benefits. This win-win philosophy does not yet fit with the zero-sum approach still embedded in Russian official thinking. Whether in politics or in business, the Russians are deal makers who pursue and respect a hard-headed approach, not one based on sentiment. Where it suits their interests, they are ready to deal very realistically with others. We should do likewise. "Pragmatic engagement" should be our rubric, not strategic partnership.

The essence of pragmatic engagement should be to cooperate as closely as possible in the many and important areas where we have shared or overlapping interests. These will vary, but at the present time clearly include combating international terrorism; counterproliferation; climate change; inhibiting trade in narcotics; and stabilizing the Middle East, energy supply, and other aspects of trade and investment. This is a substantial agenda.

Global and Security Issues and Areas of Divergence

Design Western policy for Russia's long-term adjustment. The sovereignty and future of the post-Soviet states have become the fault line between Russia and the West. It is here that the corpse of the Cold War risks being exhumed. Western policy needs to be designed to help manage this process through a long period of adjustment.

It needs to be made clear that for the West this is not a zero-sum game. The West is not seeking to advance strategic interests at Russia's expense or to oppose legitimate Russian interests in these regions. It is not seeking to detach neighbors from Russia, and has no interest in encircling Russia (as some Russian politicians are prone to claim) or in

> These adversaries who say that Russia does not belong in the G-8 . . . are stuck in the previous century, all these Sovietologists. Despite the fact that the Soviet Union has ceased to exist, they are still there because they do not have another occupation . . . Everyone who talks about this can just talk. The dog barks, the caravan rolls on.
>
> —President Vladimir V. Putin
> January 31, 2006

neo-containment—for the simple reason that there is no need and no cause for such a policy. The West's prime interest is in the stability of the regions neighboring Russia (some of which also neighbor the EU). This ought to be Russia's prime interest, too.

Stability can best be achieved by ensuring that the sovereignty and right of the states concerned freely to determine their own future are inviolable; that ethnic and border conflicts within and between them are resolved through negotiation, not force; and that they are able to develop their governance, institutions, and economies. It is the belief of Trilateral countries that these countries would be best served by the growth of democracy; but this cannot be imposed, and the ideal must be tempered by the reality of the history, traditions, and culture of, especially, the Central Asian states, where fully functioning democracy is at best a very remote prospect. It is in everyone's interests that, on a sovereign basis free from interference and bullying, Russia's neighbors should enjoy harmonious and productive relations with Moscow.

Four of the post-Soviet states are currently a source of tension between Russia and the West:

- **Belarus.** Aleksandr Lukashenko was reelected fraudulently (there is no way of telling how he would have fared in a fair election) and has a long record of abusing human rights, but he continues to enjoy Russian protection. Until the Lukashenko dictatorship is ended, the Trilateral countries will not be able to have normal relations with Belarus. Thereafter they should give primacy to the wishes of the Belarusian people—when they are able to express them freely. If the Belarusians freely and without coercion were to choose to unite or merge with the Russian Federation, the Trilateral countries would have no justification for opposing this. If, on the other hand, Belarus, as an independent state, sought to forge a closer relationship with the EU, perhaps with a view to eventual membership, the EU should respond positively. It has no need to try to attract Belarus into the union but would have no rational basis for turning Belarus away, should it at some distant point meet the criteria, especially as neighbors such as Poland and Lithuania are inside the EU.

- **Ukraine.** Principles similar to those in Belarus should apply in Ukraine. The West should oppose Russian coercion of Ukraine, not because it seeks to capture Ukraine or has strategic designs on the country, but in order to uphold the sovereign right of the Ukrainians to determine their own future. The EU has sat on the fence over Ukraine's eligibility for membership. It should cease using weasel words and state clearly that it recognizes Ukraine as a European country (no less so than others now in the queue) and would be ready to consider an application—at a point when Ukraine is ready to meet the criteria and so long as this is the democratic wish of a clear majority of the electorate. NATO should do the same. But what the EU and NATO should not do is apply coercion of their own or engage in a geostrategic game with Russia over the heads of the Ukrainian people. It should not be a Western objective artificially to accelerate the integration of states such as Ukraine into the EU and NATO; instead the West should defend the right of the Ukrainians to make a free decision. Opinion surveys in Ukraine suggest that there is no clear majority yet for EU membership, and a clear majority against NATO accession. On any assessment, it will be a long time before Ukraine is in a position to meet the necessary conditions. Forcing the pace would play into the hands of hard-liners in Ukraine and Russia.
- **Georgia.** Georgia's history since independence has been unenviable. It has suffered from internal conflict, continuous Russian interference, Western inattention, and incompetent and corrupt government. The administration of President Saakashvili, carried to power on a wave of popular support, has disappointed the hopes vested in it for more honest and democratic government and bet-

> The collapse of the Soviet Union was a major geopolitical disaster of the century.
>
> —President Vladimir V. Putin
> April 25, 2005

ter management of the country's problems. The West should not encourage the delusion that the solution to Georgia's problems lies through NATO or EU membership. It is hard to imagine circumstances in which Georgia could properly qualify for either organization within a time span of many years or could make a meaningful contribution to them; and NATO should think long and hard before even contemplating a footprint in such a fraught and sensitive area as the Caucasus. This is not a step to be taken lightly or frivolously. The Trilateral countries should firmly support Georgian sovereignty and equally firmly encourage attention to internal stability and institution building, a rational approach to relations with Russia and negotiated resolution of the frozen conflicts.

- **Uzbekistan.** The West does not have an untarnished record in Uzbekistan. Uzbekistan's support and willingness to accept the basing of U.S. forces played a crucial part in the operation to oust the Taliban in Afghanistan. The Russian government was supportive, on the understanding that the bases were needed only for a short term. In the interests of realpolitik, Western governments turned a blind eye to the dictatorial behavior of the Karimov regime, until they were forced to take a different attitude by the Andijan massacres. Since Andijan, Karimov has made common cause with Russia and China and has ordered U.S. forces out. This certainly represents a change in the Russian, as well as the Uzbek, stance, but to suggest, as some do, that it is a change in the Russian attitude to terrorism is to oversimplify a complex set of issues. More accurately, it reflects Russian opportunism and hypersensitivity to Western, especially American, military activity around Russia's fringes. In Uzbekistan, as throughout Central Asia, it is unrealistic to envisage a flowering of Western-style democracy in any measurable timescale. A more practical approach would be to build up economic links and seek to play a constructive role in countering instability, terrorism, and drug trafficking in the region while also paying close attention to respect for human rights obligations.

Insufficient attention is being paid to Central Asia. The EU, in particular, should devote more resources to the region, as a 2006 report by the International Crisis Group has recommended.[3] The continuing conflict in Afghanistan is adding to existing pressures on regional stability. There is competition between Russian and Chinese interests in Central Asia. The Western and Asian powers should not seek to compete there with Russia and China but to forge a basis for cooperation to promote stable development.

Support Russia in the North Caucasus if Russia shifts its focus. On Chechnya and the North Caucasus, we have set out in the preceding chapter the approach that we believe would lie in Russia's best interests. We think the international community should be alive to the risk that conflict may become more extensive through the region of the North Caucasus. The international community should be ready to give active support to Russia, to the extent that the Russian government is receptive and is ready to adopt policies that respect human rights and international humanitarian law and that are geared to a broad approach to conflict resolution rather than solely to draconian use of force.

Promote a more sophisticated approach to Russia's energy security. Russia is a significant supplier to the world energy market, especially to former Soviet states and the EU; and Russia can have a large influence on price levels in the market. However, the market does not literally depend on Russia because there are alternative sources, albeit more expensive. The reality is that there is a high level of mutual interdependence. Russia depends heavily on energy exports. Russian energy companies depend on external finance. For future production, Russia will need to exploit resources in more remote areas and will need external technology and partnership with foreign energy and oil field service companies. This interdependence offers a self-evident basis for a market-led approach, under clear and transparent rules on all sides, whereby Russian companies could extend their activities more widely on the international market (Gazprom, for example, has de-

3 *Central Asia: What Role for the European Union?* Asia Report no. 113 (Bishkek/Brussels: International Crisis Group, April 10, 2006).

clared its interest in downstream acquisitions) while Russia benefits from investment by multinational companies.

Recognize overlapping interests in the Middle East. Our interests overlap in the Middle East, including in Iran. Sensible handling of Iran and other Middle Eastern problems risks becoming a casualty of the deteriorating Russo-Western relationship. As a neighbor of Iran (in the sensitive Caspian and Caucasus region) and a substantial trading partner, Russia has interests and a perspective not identical with those of Western Europe or the United States. Russia has a strong interest in an outcome that would be peaceful and would avoid the emergence of another nuclear-armed state on its borders. Western policy makers need to recognize this interest and work with Russia to find solutions, but they should not have to pay a price for Russian cooperation where it is manifestly in Russia's interests to work for the same outcome.

Welcome improved Russia-China relations. The improvement in relations between Russia and China should be generally welcomed. Only a generation ago, there was intermittent conflict between these two huge powers. It is far better for the world that they should be friends, having resolved their border dispute. There is a large degree of complementarity between their economies. Deeper cooperation, including the investment of Chinese human and material resources in the development of eastern Russia, would be a rational step. It would help to build confidence and underpin a more stable relationship in the future. On some issues, the closer relationship between China and Russia will turn out to be inconvenient to the interests of Trilateral countries, but this does not make it illegitimate. We should not overreact when this happens, or naively assume that Russia will take the side of the West when the latter is in disagreement with China. Nor is it illegitimate for Russia to supply armaments to China. Russia is not in breach of any United Nations sanctions. It inherited a huge defense industry from the USSR. With the end of the Cold War, it has lost many of its traditional markets to Western suppliers. China (followed by India) is by far Russia's largest remaining market for defense equipment, its largest manufactured export. The Russians have evidently decided that they cannot afford to forgo exports worth billions, despite their own concerns about China's military buildup. Some Russian politicians like to taunt the West and Japan with the notion that Russia might team up with China in an anti-Western axis. If our analysis is correct, the wariness and suspicion between these two neighbors (indeed, for many

Russians, fear) and the strength of their separate interests in and with the West, including trade, make this an improbable scenario. It is more likely that, over time, nervousness about China's growing power could impel Russia to seek closer relations with the West.

Encourage Russia to enhance its cooperation with leading economies and advanced democracies. Russia's membership and chairmanship of the G-8, which we reviewed in chapter 5, has been called in question. Russia plainly is not one of the world's eight leading economies and advanced democracies. It has disappointed the hopes vested in it when the decisions were taken on admission and chairmanship. But Russia's membership is a fact and, short of an outrage occurring, the decision to include Russia will not be reversed. To do so would be to create a very deep rift, in no one's best interests. Attention should therefore be focused, as we suggest in the earlier chapter, on how best to use the G-8 summit to encourage Russia to return to a more cooperative path and on how to handle it so that the summit is not falsely presented as a seal of approval.

The controversy over Russian membership should also stimulate further thought about the future of the G-8, which, as we have noted, is not to be taken for granted. The G-8 is not a formal international institution, and it has no legal status or powers. That of itself makes Russia's anomalous membership an easier proposition. Since the group first began 31 years ago at an informal get-together of six leaders to discuss the world economy, it has proved to be an intermittently useful tool, essentially for high-level brainstorming and coordination. Russia's accession broadened the group beyond its origins as a small club of the West and Japan. Rather than seek to remove Russia or to wind the club up, there is a strong case now for the G-8 to institute, under the next chair (the German chancellor), a review of its purposes and methods. This could include the question of whether the membership should be broadened. China and India are obvious candidates (with a case also for thinking, perhaps at a later stage, about South Africa and Brazil). Ten members (actually eleven, as the EU also attends) would not be unmanageable. To those who argue that enlargement would change the nature of the event, we would say that it has already changed, thanks to Russia.

Instruments of Engagement

Reinforce mutually advantageous cooperation. Seeking to isolate or punish Russia, or to withdraw cooperation, would bring no benefit to the interests of the Trilateral countries. It would play into the hands of backward-looking isolationist elements within Russia. Far from thinking along such unproductive lines, we need, to the extent possible, to reinforce the channels through which we can foster mutually advantageous cooperation and narrow the ignorance gap, mentioned above. Six channels are especially important:

- **Business.** With politics in stagnation, as we have argued in the preceding chapter, business has become potentially the most dynamic force for change in Russia. It attracts the young elite and interacts with the outside world; in a growing number of companies, it requires conformity with international standards of law, accountancy, and governance. Wider interaction—business partnerships, Russian entry into rules-based foreign markets, IPOs, shareholder pressure—will have a beneficial influence on all concerned. Trilateral governments and businesses should actively encourage this process, with the proviso that the rules of fair competition should apply equally to all actors. Trilateral governments should do all they can to promote open markets, the education and training of young Russian businesspeople, and interchange between businesspeople at all levels. This would be to mutual advantage, commercially and more widely. The freeing of trade can be a motor for change.
- **Information.** This is best left to market forces and the private sector, although there is a small role for governments, for example, in supporting broadcasting. The rapid dissemination of information has acquired such importance in the global economy that any attempt to constrict it by the Russian authorities would be not only highly unpopular but also damaging to Russian economic interests. Nevertheless, Trilateral governments need to be vigilant in defending the flow of information to and from Russia and should take very seriously any interference with it.
- **Travel.** From a standing start, Russia has become one of the world's main exporters of tourism. Russians are also traveling abroad on business in large numbers. Their exit from the country is not impeded, but getting a visa to enter Western countries is

often not straightforward, especially for those outside the elite. Some countries refuse up to half the applications they receive, others as few as 5 percent, while others no longer demand visas from Russians. These are procedures worth keeping under constant review. Facilitating travel by Russians to other countries is one of the most obvious ways of helping them experience the benefits of modern and democratic societies.

- **Education.** Along with business, education should be the most significant instrument for bridging the gap over the next generation. Where there are resources available, there can be no better use of them than in sustaining and expanding the volume of educational interchange between Russia and the Trilateral countries. This can be effected at different levels, from school pupils to postgraduates and professionals, and in different ways, including delivery of education by international institutions within Russia. Some countries, notably but not only the United States, have been generous in funding exchanges. The Russian government has also played a part, through scholarship schemes and a presidential program. The results can be seen in the success of young Russians who have benefited from educational experience abroad. If we are concerned about Russia's future, these various efforts should be redoubled.
- **Opinion formers and policy makers.** The spotlight of international attention has moved away from Russia, and a degree of Russia fatigue has set in abroad. In consequence, the level of interchange between opinion formers—parliamentarians, media figures, policy experts, academics—has declined. So, therefore, has the level of understanding. One finding from our consultations for this report was that the circuit of experts in Russia and the Trilateral area who meet to exchange views has become very narrow. Expertise is strongest and best resourced in the United States; it is thin in Asia; and it has become surprisingly weak in much of Europe. Given the scale and importance of the EU-Russia relationship, Europe would benefit from a better-connected network of expertise, linking with opinion in the United States and elsewhere and developing exchanges and contacts with a wider group of Russians than is currently the case.
- **NGOs.** There are estimated to be more than 300,000 NGOs of one kind or another in Russia. Most are small and purely indigenous, but some have benefited enormously from links with com-

parable organizations in other countries. This has certainly been the case in the broad area of learning about democratic practices, of which Russia had no previous experience, but international contact and best practices have been no less important in the social sector, for example in dealing with disability, homelessness, alcoholism, domestic violence, and a wide range of health-care problems. For such activity to be conducted by independent groups and associations is new to Russia; in Soviet times, it was handled exclusively under state or Communist Party control. As we have noted in the report, the urge to control civil society and NGOs, and suspicion about international contacts, has returned. We should do all we can to prevent unfounded suspicions from preventing normal and transparent support and encouragement being given to people who are working to improve life in their own country.

Endpiece

The year 2006 is not the easiest time to be advocating engagement with Russia—albeit engagement, as we have argued, grounded on mutual interests, with less starry-eyed rhetoric, fewer unrealizable ambitions, a firm approach to principles and standards, and a realistic appreciation of Russia's direction of travel. Russia is moving into a tense and difficult period as the Duma and presidential elections, of late 2007 and early 2008, respectively, approach.

The 2008 U.S. presidential election is beginning to cast its shadow. Leaders will be changing within this period also in Japan, the UK, and France. The conflicts in Iraq and Afghanistan are a major preoccupation, as is Iran's aspiration to nuclear status. The high price of oil imposes its own pressures. All of these have the capacity to complicate the management of relations with Russia.

Notwithstanding these distractions, and the negative tone that has entered into the relationship with Russia of late, it is the common view of the three coauthors, from three continents, that the best interests of their regions will be served by pursuing a patient, long-term, and, to the extent possible, constructive policy of engagement. As they have stressed throughout the report, they see this as a task for a generation or more, from which we should not be deflected by twists, turns, and bumps along the way. Above all, engagement with Russia should not just, or even primarily, be a matter of engagement with state actors at

> Perhaps even the rational Westerner has to conclude that it does after all help to judge Russia by the light of faith as well as reason. Faith, a dash of hope, and some of that charitable understanding which Russians have not often enjoyed from those who look in on them from outside.
>
> —Rodric Braithwaite
> *Across the Moscow River,* 2002

the highest level. The most effective contribution that the outside world can make to Russia will be to use the many opportunities that now exist to engage with as wide a range of people and organizations as possible.